The Water Crisis
Constructing Solutions to Freshwater Pollution

BLACK
ROSE
BOOKS

Montréal/New York
London

Black Rose Books No. CC278
Hardcover ISBN: 1-55164-145-3 (bound)
Paperback ISBN: 1-55164-144-5 (pbk.)

Canadian Cataloguing in Publication Data
Stauffer, Julie
Water crisis : finding the right solutions

Includes bibliographical references and index.
Hardcover ISBN: 1-55164-145-3(bound)
Paperback ISBN: 1-55164-144-5 (pbk.)

1. Water—Pollution. I. Title.

TD420.S72 1999   363.739'4   C99-900750-5

Cover Design by Associés libres, Montréal

BLACK ROSE BOOKS

C.P. 1258	2250 Military Road	99 Wallis Road
Succ. Place du Parc	Tonawanda, New York	London, E9 5LN
Montréal, H2W 2R3	14150	England
Canada	USA	UK

To order books in North America:
(phone) 1-800-565-9523 (fax) 1-800-221-9985
In Europe: (phone) 0181-986-4854 (fax) 0181-533-5821

Our Web Site address: http://www.web.net/blackrosebooks
A publication of the Institute of Policy Alternatives of Montréal (IPAM)
Printed in Canada

The Canada Council for the Arts
Le Conseil des Arts du Canada

Contents

PART III: SOLUTIONS

PART IV: GROUND-WATER

PART V: CONCLUSIONS

List of Tables

List of Boxes

List of Figures

Introduction

Clean, plentiful water is infinitely precious – without it we could not survive. Yet we use our waterways as a dumping ground for waste, pouring billions of tonnes of chemicals, metals and organic pollutants into lakes, rivers and oceans every year. Almost two centuries ago, Benjamin Franklin said that we do not know the true value of water until the well runs dry. Today we continue to ignore the vital importance of water, while consuming more and more. Not only is the level of water in the global well getting low, the water is also polluted, sometimes to the point where it is no longer drinkable.

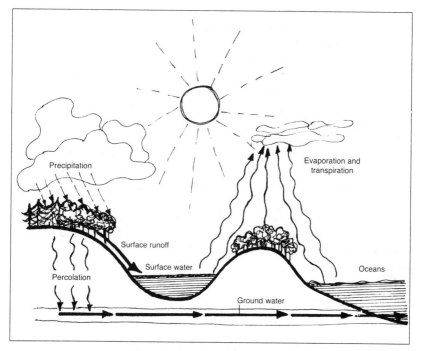

Figure I.1 *The Water Cycle*

We need clean water. Nor are humans the only ones to depend on it. Fish, animals, plants – all life relies on clean water. Water is essential for drinking, irrigation, industrial activity and recreation, but it is a recycled resource. It moves constantly through the ecosphere, collecting in the atmosphere as clouds, falling to earth as rain or snow, percolating into underground reservoirs, and flowing into lakes, rivers and seas. The circle becomes complete when it evaporates back into the atmosphere, forming clouds once again (see Figure I.1).

Whenever we contaminate one part of this cycle, we risk contaminating it all. For example, DDT, a pesticide now banned in most developed countries, has been detected in every phase of the water cycle. What we pour down the drain comes back out of our tap. For all these reasons, we need to protect and restore the quality of our water.

This book examines many of the issues of water pollution. Part I describes the three biggest contributors to modern water pollution: urbanization, industrialization and intensive agriculture. It looks at where pollutants come from, and what effect they have. These issues are illustrated by two major case-studies: the Rhine River in Europe and the Great Lakes in North America. Part II discusses how to prevent water pollution. Part III explores innovative, ecological technologies that clean and restore polluted waste-water. Part IV discusses some of the special problems presented by ground-water pollution.

The topic is a broad one. I've narrowed it to pollution of fresh water, and have focussed specifically on freshwater pollution in developed countries where, hopefully, there are sufficient resources to tackle the problem. Even so, this book is only an overview, illustrating the nature and scope of the problems, and, most importantly, of the solutions. While the threats to our water are real, the tools to tackle them exist, and are being used. Read on.

Part I

Problems

Chapter 1

Urbanization:
Sewage and Storm-water

For as long as humans have lived together in settlements, they have had an impact on their environment. Trees are cut down to make room for houses, roads are built, and wells are dug or streams are diverted to provide drinking-water. By far the biggest impact, however, is caused by human waste disposal. The larger and more dense the settlement, the bigger and more concentrated the problem. With the development of flush toilets, things really got out of hand.

For thousands of years, the flush toilet didn't exist. People used 'conservancy' systems, such as earth closets, pit privies and cesspools, which return human waste to the land. The earth closet was basically a wooden seat with a bucket underneath. A hopper behind the seat contained dry earth, charcoal or ashes that emptied into the bucket when you pulled a handle. When the bucket became full, you replaced it with an empty one. The full buckets were collected regularly and transported to farms, where the contents were used as fertilizer.

Other popular systems included pit privies and cesspools. A pit privy was essentially a hole in the ground with a seat on top (and walls around it for privacy). Waste fell into the hole, where soil organisms went to work, breaking down the solid organic material. The liquid percolated into the surrounding soil. When the hole became full, you dug a new one. Cesspools stored human waste, but unlike pit privies, they didn't treat it. They were lined, water-tight pits that had to be emptied frequently, and their contents transported elsewhere for disposal.

Conservancy systems were used for thousands of years. It was only in the last century that they were replaced by the now-familiar water carriage system.

The Water Carriage Revolution

Water carriage has three basic components: a water closet (WC) or flush toilet that flushes your waste, sewers that carry away what you've flushed, and some form of disposal and possibly treatment of the waste at the other end of the sewers. Clearly it necessitates a lot more infrastructure than the conservancy system, and this didn't appear overnight. The water carriage revolution took place relatively slowly, piece by piece, beginning with the invention of the WC.

DEVELOPMENT OF THE WC

Although many societies have built latrines that emptied into water-courses, and even diverted watercourses to run underneath latrines, the first modern flushing toilet was not invented until 1596 by Sir John Harrington. However, his toilet had a number of weaknesses, including the lack of a water trap that prevented sewer odours from reaching the user's nose, and (understandably) it did not catch on. Almost 200 years later, improved versions of the WC were designed independently by Cumming and Bramah. Their inventions included all the basic features of a modern flush toilet: flushing water, a holding tank, a flushing valve, an overhead supply and siphon and, perhaps most importantly, a water trap (see Figure 1.1). This time, the world proved more receptive.

WCs offered several advantages over earth closets. They were cleaner and had fewer offensive odours. They flushed waste away, instead of leaving it to decompose. Finally, although WCs were expensive to install, water carriage was ultimately cheaper than paying someone with a horse and cart to collect and haul earth buckets. Beginning in the early nineteenth century, water carriage slowly gained ascendency over the conservancy system. There were two particularly compelling reasons for this shift: the increasing volume of urban waste, and the disease that accompanied it.

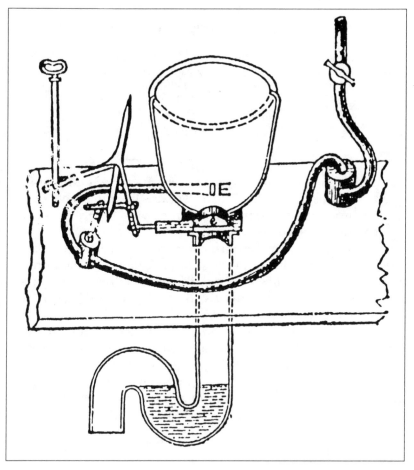

Figure 1.1 *Cumming's Toilet*

In the UK, the Industrial Revolution brought an influx of labourers from the country to the city to work in the newly created factories. Urban populations boomed, and demand for fertilizer in the country could no longer keep up with the increased urban supply of human waste. As more waste was produced in the cities, and as it had to be transported further and further to the farms, the conservancy system became uneconomic.

At the same time, most towns weren't prepared for the consequences of this population influx. Workers lived in shanty towns where there was no provision for removing domestic wastes. Excrement collected in courtyards, alleyways and streets, and diseases were spread by personal contact and by flies. Wells became contaminated by human wastes seeping from overloaded privies and cesspools, spreading even more disease. In these working class areas, diarrhoea, gastroenteritis, dysentery, typhoid fever, and paratyphoid fever were endemic.

WCs solved many of these problems. Waste was flushed away instead of being left to rot, significantly reducing the spread of disease. In Nottingham, for example, the Medical Officer of Health found that the rate of enteric fever was 50 per cent lower in areas of the town served by WCs than in areas served by earth closets, and 14 times lower than in areas served by pit privies.

SANITARY SEWERS

The real impetus for change came with the cholera epidemics that swept through the UK in 1831–32 and 1848–49, killing thousands of people. Sir Edwin Chadwick, the famous sanitary campaigner, blamed the unhygienic conditions in most manufacturing towns for the rapid spread of cholera. He strongly advocated a change from the conservancy system to a water carriage system for removing human waste. He also advocated the construction of sewers. At that time, many towns did not have sewers, and those sewers that did exist were intended for storm-water, not human waste. Most WCs discharged their wastes into cesspools and privy vaults which, because they were not designed to deal with the large volumes of liquid waste created by flush toilets, were in constant danger of overflowing. Chadwick fought against the restrictions that prohibited disposing of domestic waste into storm-water sewers, and suggested instead an 'arterial system of drainage' (Chadwick, quoted in Finer, 1952; pp 214–216) where sewers transported both storm-water and domestic sewage. His proposals were approved, and the water carriage revolution began in earnest.

Thus, in the UK, sanitary sewers were developed as a direct result of the cholera epidemics that swept the nation. This was also true in Paris, where sewers were constructed in response to the 1832 epidemic. However, a slightly different story unfolded in the US. Cholera never struck hard there, but two important factors paved the way towards sanitary sewers. As urban populations expanded, and as more and more people gained access to piped water, household water consumption increased rapidly. At the same time, the WC was gaining popularity, adding further to water consumption. The resulting waste-water overwhelmed cesspools and privies designed to handle more modest volumes, creating serious flooding problems and threatening to contaminate water supplies. Private citizens, engineers and public health officials all pressured municipalities to construct sanitary sewers.

Ironically, sewers created their own public health threats. In the nineteenth century, sewage treatment didn't exist; sewers simply carried wastes to the most convenient place for disposal – often the nearest watercourse. At the time, engineers believed that 'running water purified itself' (Sedgwick, 1918; pp 213, 231–237), so dumping raw sewage into rivers and lakes was not a danger to downstream cities. Not surprisingly, this theory proved false. Although a river can assimilate a certain amount of organic waste, it can't cope with huge volumes of sewage, and it can't destroy every pathogen present in human waste. For example, 50 per cent of typhoid bacteria are destroyed in an aquatic environment in 1–3 days; 90 per cent are destroyed in 3–13 days; but the most resistant can live for many weeks and still retain their power of infection.

The results of relying on the assimilative capacity of rivers and lakes to treat sewage were major outbreaks of typhoid fever in downstream cities and highly polluted waterways. At first, municipalities responded by filtering and chlorinating their drinking supplies, and continued to discharge raw sewage. Chicago went so far as to actually reverse the flow of the Chicago River so that it drained into the Illinois River, rather than Lake Michigan, which supplied the city's drinking-water. But typhoid rates remained high, and it was not until sewage treatment became widespread that the disease was brought under control.

In the UK, the introduction of the water carriage system greatly improved the standard of living for the urban working class: conditions became much more sanitary, and the level of disease dropped. However, at the same time, water carriage severely degraded the quality of the nation's rivers. As early as 1867, English civil engineer Baldwin Latham pointed out that 'the lives and health of our citizens have been purchased at the expense of the rivers' (Latham, 1867).

There are three basic components of sewage that create the environmental damage: suspended solids, organic material and nutrients.

Suspended Solids

Suspended solids are small particles in sewage. If they are not removed, they will cloud the receiving water, preventing sunlight from penetrating into the water column. This impairs the growth of aquatic plants and algae, and thus depletes the amount of food available for fish. In addition, some fish species such as northern pike and trout rely on sight in order to feed, and they cannot survive in highly turbid water. When the particles settle out, they can suffocate bottom-dwelling organisms and silt up fish spawning grounds.

Organic Material

The largest component of sewage (aside from water) is organic material, measured by its biochemical oxygen demand (BOD). As organic material breaks down, it uses up or 'demands' oxygen. This has serious consequences for aquatic organisms that need oxygen to live. The more organic material you throw in a lake, the more oxygen it takes to break it down, and the unhappier the fish in the

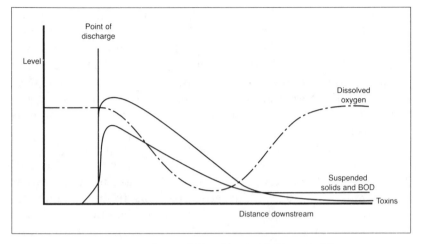

Figure 1.2 *Effect of Sewage Outfall on a River*

lake are going to be as there is progressively less oxygen for them to breathe.

Organic material occurs naturally in aquatic environments: fish die, leaves fall into streams and soil washes into rivers. This kind of material is fairly insoluble, however. It breaks down quite slowly, so it does not demand a lot of oxygen all at once. It's a different picture when you pour thousands of litres of sewage into a lake. Because sewage is made up of lots of small bits of organic material dissolved or suspended in water, it starts to break down very quickly, creating an immediate demand for large amounts of oxygen. Furthermore, as it breaks down, reduction as well as oxidation can occur. When organic material is reduced, it liberates ammonia. Neither oxygen depletion nor ammonia liberation is good for fish or other aquatic organisms. For example, salmon and trout require a minimum oxygen level of 6 milligrams per litre to live in a river. Trout cannot grow if the ammonia concentration exceeds 0.025 milligrams per litre, and they will die if it exceeds 0.25 milligrams per litre.

The biggest impact is immediately downstream from a sewage outfall, where the organic matter starts decomposing, using up oxygen and releasing ammonia (see Figure 1.2). Further downstream, the effect is smaller. The concentration of organic matter decreases as some of it breaks down into carbon dioxide and nutrients, and the rest of it gets diluted. Ammonia levels are therefore lower and oxygen levels are higher. The further the distance downstream from the outfall, the smaller the effect becomes, as bacteria transform the ammonia to nitrate and oxygen enters the water from the atmosphere. This process of recovery is called 'self-purification' or 'assimilation'.

Whenever the volume of organic matter entering a body of water exceeds the capacity of the body to purify or assimilate it, there is a problem. Even if the volume of organic matter is within the assimilative capacity, it can cause problems. In the area immediately around the outfall, the water will be low in oxygen and high in ammonia. In a small river, this can be enough to prevent fish from swimming upstream to spawn.

Nitrogen and Phosphorus

Aquatic plants (like any other plants) need two essential nutrients to grow: nitrogen and phosphorus. In small quantities, these nutrients are good. In large quantities, they can cause a major water pollution problem: excessive nutrients are one of the biggest contributors to surface-water pollution in the US. Too many nutrients stimulate the rapid growth of plants and algae, clogging waterways and sometimes creating blooms of toxic blue–green algae, a process known as eutrophication. Then, as these plants and algae eventually die and decompose, they use up large amounts of oxygen, reducing the amount available for fish and other aquatic species. In extreme cases, this can lead to a completely oxygenless environment that can support nothing except a few species of anaerobic bacteria.

Sewage has a very high nitrogen content, due largely to the presence of urine. It also contains phosphorous – about half occurs naturally in human waste, the other half comprises phosphates from laundry detergent. Phosphorus occurs in many different forms, often lumped together under the heading 'total phosphorus'. Aquatic plants need both nitrogen and phosphorus to grow. Phosphorus is usually the one in shortest supply, making it a limiting nutrient. Plant growth is thus determined by the amount of

10

phosphorus in the water; the more phosphorus gets into the water, the more the plants will grow. So to control eutrophication, it is essential to reduce phosphorus pollution.

Other Contaminants

In the past two centuries, disposing of human waste has been complicated by the presence of other pollutants such as oils, petrols, chemicals and heavy metals – the byproducts of modern civilization. These are discussed in more detail in subsequent chapters.

SEWAGE TREATMENT

So sewage treatment became necessary to protect both human health and the health of surface-waters. Modern treatment methods were developed around the turn of the century and subsequently improved.

The first step in modern treatment methods is preliminary treatment to remove grit and larger material that could damage the treatment plant's machinery (see Figure 1.3). In this stage, the waste-water enters channels designed to slow its velocity enough to settle out grit. Next, it passes through bar screens that remove debris such as sticks and rags. After preliminary treatment, the waste-water enters large primary settling tanks, where the velocity is further slowed, allowing suspended solids to settle to the bottom, forming a layer of sludge. Primary treatment removes roughly 50 per cent of the suspended solids (see Table 1.1).

Secondary treatment relies on bacterial action to remove most of the remaining suspended and dissolved organic material. This can take different forms. In larger urban areas, the most common method is activated sludge treatment, a process that involves bubbling large volumes of air into the waste-water to encourage bacterial action. The bacteria occur naturally in sewage, and, in the presence of oxygen, they feed on the organic matter and break it down. When the waste-water passes into secondary settling tanks, the bacteria (and the solids they've ingested) settle to the bottom as sludge. A portion of this sludge is recycled back into the aeration tanks to ensure a large population of bacteria.

In smaller towns, a clinker bed may be used for secondary treatment. In this system, the waste-water is poured over a bed of small stone fragments. The stones become coated with a naturally occurring film of bacteria that breaks down the dissolved organic material.

This still leaves nutrients and pathogens in the waste-water. Nutrients can be removed by using tertiary treatment. In this process, ammonia and organic nitrogen are removed by nitrification/denitrification: first they are transformed to nitrate in the presence of oxygen, and then they are denitrified to nitrogen gas in the absence of oxygen. Phosphorus can be removed chemically by adding lime, aluminium or iron salts, which form compounds that precipitate out of the waste-water.

The final stage of waste-water treatment is disinfection, which kills harmful bacteria and viruses. Most commonly this is accomplished by adding chlorine, but in recent years there has been concern about some of the side-effects of this process. Chlorine can react with organic material to form dangerous organochlorine compounds. A number of studies (Government of Canada, 1993) found that chlorinated waste-water effluent is acutely lethal to fish in the area immediately around a sewage treatment plant outfall, and causes changes in the aquatic community further downstream. Canada now classifies chlorinated waste-water effluent as toxic. Likewise, in the UK, the National Rivers Authority decided that 'there is clear evidence that "List I" dangerous substances are created by chlorine sewage disinfection, and the UK is committed to the elimination of these substances from the water environment' (*ENDS Report*, 1992, pp 11–12). These effects could be reduced or eliminated by dechlorinating the effluent before releasing it, by adding sulphur dioxide, sodium metabisulphite, sodium bisulphite, sodium thiosulphite or hydrogen peroxide, or by using activated carbon.

There are also alternatives to chlorination that do not create harmful compounds, methods such as ultraviolet (UV) radiation and ozonation. UV radiation is generated by light bulbs that are immersed in the waste-water. It works by damaging the DNA of harmful viruses and bacteria as the sewage flows past. For this method to work effectively, the waste-water must be relatively clean (too many suspended solids will block the UV rays), and the flow

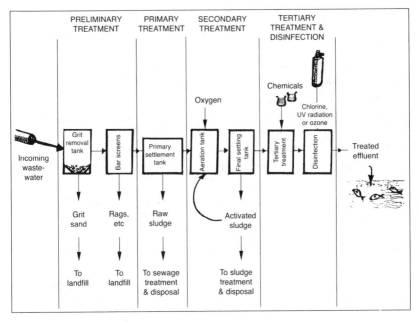

Figure 1.3 *Conventional Treatment*

must be carefully controlled so the bulbs are immersed in waste-water at all times. The costs of a UV radiation system are similar to those of chlorination/dechlorination.

Ozone is a powerful, reliable oxidant that kills bacteria and viruses. It is generated on-site by passing air or pure oxygen through an electrical discharge. Ozonation is more expensive than UV radiation or chlorination/dechlorination because it requires large amounts of energy. Like UV radiation, ozonation demands that the waste-water has undergone at least secondary treatment.

Treatment plants are now left with two products: clean waste-water, which is ready to be discharged into the nearest body of water, and the semi-liquid sludge that is produced during primary and secondary settling. There are a number of options for disposing of the sludge, including incineration, ocean dumping, landfill or application to land. These are discussed in more detail in Chapter 8. In summary, conventional sewage treatment plants speed up natural bacterial action by adding lots of oxygen and enclose it all in a concrete infrastructure. The process is fast and takes up relatively little room, but the construction and operation costs are high.

Although the first sewage treatment plants were built during the early years of this century, it is only in the past few decades that most towns and cities in the Western world have acquired them. Sewage treatment has had an enormous beneficial impact: from the late 1970s to the late 1980s, BOD levels in Europe and North America decreased by 75 per cent. However, the absence of sewage treatment plants remains a serious problem in many areas. This means that nutrients, ammonia, organic material, microorganisms and toxins pour into local bodies of water. In Albania there are no sewage treatment plants at all; untreated domestic and industrial sewage is discharged directly into rivers and the Mediterranean. Much of central, eastern and southern Europe does not have adequate numbers of sewage treatment plants.

Even where treatment plants exist, the degree of treatment can vary significantly (see Table 1.2). Some plants provide only primary treatment, while very few provide tertiary treatment. Futhermore, many plants are ageing or overloaded and no longer perform optimally. In 1990, 15 per cent of treatment plants in large US cities significantly contravened their discharge requirements, while in the UK the number is closer to 20 per cent.

Table 1.1 *Comparison of Effectiveness of Primary, Secondary and Tertiary Treatment (Percentage Removal)*

Constituent	Primary	Secondary	Tertiary
Suspended solids	60–70	80–95	90–95
BOD	20–40	70–90	> 95
Phosphorus	10–30	20–40	85–97
Nitrogen	10–20	20–40	20–40
E. coli bacteria	60–90	90–99	> 99
Viruses	30–70	90–99	> 99
Cadmium and zinc	5–20	20–40	40–60
Copper, lead and chromium	40–60	70–90	80–89

Source: Stanners and Bourdeau (1995)

Table 1.2 *Population Served by Waste-water Treatment Plants, Most Recent Year*

Country	Total served	Primary treatment only	Not served
Canada	75.0	20.0	25.0
USA	71.6	10.8	28.4
Japan	45.9	0	54.1
Austria	72.0	5.0	28.0
Denmark	98.0	8.0	2.0
Finland	76.1	0	23.9
Germany	91.9	2.1	8.1
Greece	11.4	0.7	88.6
Iceland	6.0	6.0	94.0
Italy	60.7	0	39.3
Luxembourg	90.4	3.2	9.6
The Netherlands	93.0	1.0	7.0
Norway	57.0	13.0	43.0
Portugal	20.9	9.4	79.1
Spain	53.0	11.0	47.0
Sweden	95.0	1.0	5.0
Switzerland	91.0	0	9.0
Turkey	6.3	1.3	93.7
UK	87.0	8.0	13.0

Source: OECD (1994)

BOD is a problem wherever adequate sewage treatment is lacking, for example in central, eastern and southern Europe. A healthy level of BOD is considered to be 5 milligrams of oxygen per litre of water. In Bulgaria, BOD exceeds this level in 60 per cent of rivers; in Belgian Flanders, it is 69 per cent of rivers; and in Romania, a staggering 80 per cent.

Urban Runoff

Although flush toilets have created the biggest source of urban water pollution, pavement also plays a signficant role. In urban areas, much of the land is sealed off by rooftops, driveways, roads and car parks, creating an impermeable surface. Normally, when rain falls on the earth, it is absorbed by the soil. Some of it gets taken up by vegetation, some percolates into ground-water, and some slowly makes its way into surfacewater. Paving and building over land changes all this. When the rain falls, it hits an impermeable surface that it is forced to flow across. As it does so, it picks up a load of urban pollutants: heavy metals from vehicle exhausts, tyre wear and corrosion of building materials; road grit; silts and sediments from construction projects; organic plant and animal material; bacteria from animal excrement; pesticides from urban lawns and parks; road salt; grease; oil; and antifreeze.

There is a complex infrastructure of drains, storm sewers and outfalls designed to funnel all this polluted storm-water off the streets as quickly as possible, so urban pedestrians don't have to wade through puddles and vehicles are not slowed down by slippery or icy roads. Usually these storm sewers deposit storm-water without treatment directly into local waterways, where it has a number of negative effects. First of all, it pollutes the streams, rivers or lakes that act as receiving bodies. Studies have found that urban runoff can contain high enough levels of copper, lead and zinc to kill many species of fish and aquatic invertebrates. It is also a major source of toxic metals, chlorinated organic compounds and suspended solids. Generally speaking, urban rivers are too contaminated to support anything but the most pollution-tolerant of fish species. Secondly, it comes as a sudden rush instead of gradually filtering through soil and vegetation. The force of the water can cause stream-bed erosion and destroy aquatic habitats, while the particles suspended in the storm-water have a scouring action. If the waterway has been straightened out and channelized, the flow of water will speed up even more, increasing the risk of flood damage. Finally, because all the storm-water is channelled into local waterways with such efficiency, there is no reserve of water filtering into streams and rivers during dry weather. Streams may dry up completely and water levels in rivers can drop dramatically. This is also damaging to aquatic habitats.

In some cities, rainfall can cause an additional headache – combined sewer overflow. Combined sewers were built as a cost-saving measure because they serve the purpose of both storm-water and sanitary sewers. During dry weather, they transport waste-water to a sewage treatment plant. However, during wet weather, they carry both waste-water and storm-water. Sometimes the resulting volumes are too much for the sewage treatment plant to handle. The excess, or combined sewer overflow, is dumped directly into the receiving water without treatment, or is given only primary treatment. Combined sewer overflow contains the combined pollutants of sewage and storm-water: BOD, pathogens, nutrients, heavy metals, pesticides, oils and suspended solids.

Finally, winter road salt is a seasonal source of pollution in northern cities, sometimes turning local waterways as salty as sea-water. Like storm-water, snow melt carries a heavy burden of pollutants, particularly from vehicle emissions. A study in Stockholm found 30,000 kilogrammes of lead, 6000 kilogrammes of oil and 130,000 kilogrammes of sodium chloride in 850,000 cubic metres of snow cleared from city streets and dumped into local receiving waters.

Chapter 2

Industrialization:
Chemical Contaminants

'Effluents are an essential by-product of modern civilization'

(Hynes, 1960; p 168)

Until the mid eighteenth century, water pollution was essentially limited to small, localized areas. Then came the coal-fired Industrial Revolution, the development of the internal combustion engine, and the petroleum-fuelled explosion of the chemical industry. Unfortunately, waste-water treatment did not keep pace. Sewage treatment plants were originally designed to remove organic matter from waste-water. They were not meant to cope with the waste products of a growing industrial sector, which were being discharged, raw, into municipal sewage. The synthetic chemical industry presented a particular challenge, creating hundreds of thousands of new chemicals.

Treatment plants are faced with many pollutants, such as dioxins, heavy metals and polychlorinated biphenols (PCBs), which they cannot treat or remove, so the chemicals pass into lakes, rivers and oceans. These can prove toxic to aquatic life, interfere with reproduction and biomagnify and bioaccumulate in the food chain. Not only are they not removed during sewage treatment, these chemicals are not removed during water treatment either, so they may also be a threat to humans who draw their drinking-water supplies from these sources. In 1974, a report by the US

Environmental Defense Fund provided the first evidence linking the high incidence of deaths from cancer to drinking-water quality (Robert Harris, cited in Shaeffer and Stevens, 1983). More recent studies suggest that some of these contaminants may also attack our immune systems, disrupt our reproductive systems or affect development in our children. Today, persistent industrial chemicals such as organohalogen compounds, polycyclic aromatic hydrocarbons, pesticides and PCBs now contaminate every step of the water cycle. They have been detected in sewage, rain-water, surface-water, ground-water, sea-water, and drinking-water supplies. We have reached the stage where the entire hydrosphere, with the possible exception of the polar ice caps, is contaminated (at least to some degree) by our industrial pollutants.

There are many types of industrial contaminants; each sector produces its own particular combination of pollutants (see Table 2.1). The metal-working industry discharges chromium, nickel, zinc, cadmium, lead, iron and titanium compounds – electroplating companies are particularly bad offenders. Photofinishing shops produce silver, dry cleaning and car body repair shops generate solvent waste, and printing plants release inks and dyes. The pulp and paper industry relies heavily on chlorine-based substances, and as a result, pulp and paper mill effluents contain dioxins and furans, as well as suspended solids and organic wastes. The petrochemical industry discharges lots of phenols and mineral oils, while waste-water from food processing plants is high in suspended solids and organic material. Industrial waste-water treatment must be designed specifically for the particular type of effluent produced.

The remainder of this chapter examines some of the most common components of industrial waste-water: suspended solids, organic material, heavy metals, synthetic chemicals and acidic wastes.

Suspended Solids

Like municipal sewage, industrial waste-water frequently contains suspended solids, or sediments. These very fine particles are discharged by food processing plants, pulp and paper mills and

19

Table 2.1 *Water Pollutants by Industrial Sector*

Sector	Pollutant
Iron and steel	BOD, COD, oil, metals, acids, phenols, and cyanide
Textiles and leather	BOD, solids, sulphates, and chromium
Pulp and paper	BOD, COD, solids, chlorinated organic compounds
Petrochemicals and refineries	BOD, COD, mineral oils, phenols, and chromium
Chemicals	COD, organic chemicals, heavy metals, SS, and cyanide
Non-ferrous metals	fluorine, SS
Microelectronics	COD, organic chemicals
Mining	SS, metals, acids, salts

COD, Chemical oxygen demand; SS, suspended solids.

ore processing industries. They silt up waterways, suffocating bottom-dwelling organisms, eliminating fish spawning areas, impeding navigation and increasing the costs of drinking-water treatment. Often they carry nutrients, heavy metals and other pollutants with them.

Box 2.1 Polluted Bottom Sediments

Polluted bottom sediments are a major problem in the Great Lakes. Until they are permanently removed, cleaned up or buried by clean materials, contaminated sediments are an ongoing source of pollution. They can be stirred up by storms, biological activity, dredging, ship movement and wave action. The US Army Corps of Engineers dredges roughly four million cubic metres per year in the Great Lakes to maintain a navigable depth of water. While one at a time these sediments could be buried in landfill sites, the Corps of Engineers is now finding that over half of the sediments are contaminated and must be disposed of as hazardous waste.

Organic Material

Industrial waste-water can also contain various types of organic material which will use up oxygen if it is released untreated into the receiving water. This is commonly measured as BOD, the amount of oxygen used up as microorganisms break down the organic material in a particular sample. Alternatively, it can be measured as chemical oxygen demand (COD), the oxygen demand created when strong chemical oxidants are used to degrade organic material. COD is generally used for samples containing compounds that can't be degraded by microorganisms.

Heavy Metals

Heavy metals pose a threat to human health. Cadmium, lead and mercury are particularly dangerous because they can interfere with hormones and reproduction, and lead also interferes with development in children. Other metals, such as copper and zinc, are less dangerous to humans but toxic to aquatic life.

Heavy metals are a long-term problem. They don't break down, and they bioaccumulate as they pass through the food chain. Contaminated plankton are eaten by small fish, which are eaten by big fish, which are eaten by humans, and at each step in the food chain the dose of toxic metals in the meal becomes greater.

As mining and industrial activity increased through the nineteenth and twentieth centuries, the production and use of heavy metals also increased significantly. This has led to high levels of heavy metal contamination in lakes and rivers. In Europe, heavy metal pollution reached a crisis point in the 1970s, and national and international regulations were created in response. The result has been big improvements in much of western Europe. Levels are still high in some rivers, particularly around mining areas and industries that use large quantities of these metals, and heavy metal contamination continues to be a severe problem in many eastern European countries, including those in the Danube basin, the Russian Federation and the Ukraine.

Box 2.2 Mercury in the Wabigoon–English River System

Mercury is a poison that attacks the central nervous system, causing loss of sensation, lack of coordination, speech and hearing impairments and tunnel vision.

In 1970, Canadian scientists discovered mercury in the Wabigoon–English River system of north-western Ontario. From 1963 to 1970, a pulp and paper plant upstream used a mercury cell to produce the chlorine used to bleach its products. Over these years, the plant discharged approximately 10 tonnes of mercury into the river.

The river system runs through Grassy Narrows and White Dog, two Ojibwe communities that relied heavily on fish for both food and income. The river poisoning was devastating for the inhabitants. Their staple source of food was toxic – studies found that fish from the river had concentrations of mercury more than 30 times the level considered safe – and residents who continued to eat large quantities of fish developed symptoms of mercury poisoning. Moreover, one of the primary sources of income for the community – guiding fishing trips – evaporated.

In the intervening years, mercury levels have decreased considerably; the concentration in crayfish, for example, has dropped by a factor of ten. However, fish from the river are still too contaminated to eat.

Source: Government of Canada (1991)

Synthetic Chemicals

There are more than ten million synthetic chemicals available today, and hundreds of new chemicals are created each week. Most are used in agriculture and industry. Some, such as phenols, ammonia, acids and sulphur, break down quickly and their effects are short-lived. Others linger in the environment for years and decades. These persistent chemicals include dioxins, furans, polychlorinated phenols and many pesticides. Like heavy metals, they can bioconcentrate and bioaccumulate in the food chain, and they are widespread. A nationwide study of freshwater fish in the US found DDT and PCBs in more than 90 per cent of samples. Many of these substances are harmful to aquatic life and to humans: organochlorines, for example, can cause cancer, suppress immune systems and disrupt hormones. Others we simply know very little about. Less than 2 per cent are sufficiently tested to provide a complete

Box 2.3 Hormone Copycats

Hormones work by attaching to a receptor in a cell and triggering some kind of response. For example, the female sex hormone oestrogen stimulates the development of breasts, among other effects. It now appears that a number of chemicals can mimic human hormones, including dioxins, PCBs, pentochlorophenol, many pesticides and certain plasticizers and surfactants. These synthetic chemicals can also attach to hormone receptors, where they can trigger a response, or block the effect of natural hormones. Either way, they disrupt reproductive systems and sometimes affect immune systems.

Many of these effects have been documented in wildlife. In the Great Lakes, herring gulls have been exposed to large quantities of such hormone copycats. They produce eggs with shells significantly thinner than normal, high numbers of chicks are born with deformities, and male chicks are born with feminized reproductive systems. In Florida, Lake Apopka is still recovering from the effects of a major pesticide spill in 1980. Today adult alligators produce almost no sex hormones – their ovaries and testes appear to be 'burnt out'. Juvenile males are feminized, and their phalluses are half the normal size. In the UK, male fish downstream from municipal sewage treatment plants have been found that produce a yolk protein normally found only in females. Researchers believe this is caused by the presence of alkyl phenols in the sewage effluent.

In humans, the links between exposure to these chemicals and hormonal disruption have not been firmly established. However, their effects could include cancer, abnormal sperm production, decreases in immune function, spontaneous abortions, hermaphroditism and sex reversal behaviour. This could account, at least in part, for the declining sperm count in men and the increased rate of breast cancer in women in most Western countries.

Source: WWF (1995)

health hazard assessment, and no health information is available for more than 70 per cent. Almost nothing is known about cumulative or synergistic effects, although we are exposed to low levels of hundreds of chemicals in our environment.

Acidic Wastes

Surface-water acidification can be due to the localized discharge of acidic effluent, or to the deposition of acid rain generated thousands of kilometres away.

MINING

The most common cause of localized acidification is mining waste. Metal and coal mines are big generators of acid effluent. Metal mining involves high levels of sulphuric acid wherever the ore, tailings or waste rock contain significant amounts of iron sulphides. The ore from which common metals are extracted can contain minerals composed of 13–50 per cent sulphur. Acidic mining effluent or acid mine drainage can take several forms: mine dewatering wastes, liquid effluents from the milling process used to extract minerals from ground ore, and surface-water drainage and seepage from waste storage areas such as unprotected piles of tailings. The effluent can be treated in settling ponds by adding lime to neutralize the acidity and increase the pH. This also precipitates out the metals as hydroxides.

One of the most controversial issues involving mine wastes is the question of who is responsible for abandoned mines. Once a mine is closed down and the pumps that prevent it from filling with water are turned off, ground-water levels will rise and flush metals out of the mine and into local waterways. Acid mine drainage pollutes almost 18,000 kilometres of streams in the US, and in England and Wales over 200 kilometres of waterways are affected by abandoned coal and metal mines.

ACID RAIN

Acid rain is a widespread and well publicized problem. It is caused by emissions from a host of sources, including coal-fired generators, petroleum refiners, iron and steel mills, pulp and paper mills and motor vehicle exhausts. These emissions contain sulphur dioxide and nitrogen oxide, which are converted to sulphuric and nitric acid in the atmosphere.

Acid rain lowers the pH of bodies of water, killing young fish and other aquatic species, and interfering in the reproduction of the surviving adults. It makes metals and other toxic substances dissolve more readily in water, causing further damage to aquatic ecosystems. At its most serious, acid rain can 'kill' lakes, eliminating most life forms. It also slows the growth of certain species of tree, and it corrodes cars and building materials.

The problem of acid rain was first noticed in the early 1970s. Scandinavia was particularly hard hit – there were several large-scale fish kills caused by acidification, and a 1980 study estimated that 18,000 lakes in Sweden alone were affected by acid rain. Any area where the underlying rock and the soil in the catchment area are poor in lime is vulnerable to acid rain, because it has no natural buffering capability. In addition to Nordic countries, Canada is very sensitive to the effects of acid rain; 14,000 Canadian lakes are considered biologically dead, and 24 bird species in eastern North America are endangered because of its impact on the food chain.

Chapter 3

Intensive Farming: Fertilizers and Pesticides

History of Modern Farming

Modern agriculture is characterized by high input techniques: mechanical tillage, chemical fertilizers and chemical pest control. While it represents a simplified and standardized approach to farming that can produce high yields, the environmental costs are also high.

The shift from traditional to intensive agriculture began between 1920 and 1950, when petrol-fuelled equipment replaced draught animals. This had a number of negative effects. First, it led to soil erosion. Because large equipment is easier to operate in large fields, farmers began removing wind breaks to accommodate the tractors, thus increasing the amount of soil blown away by wind. They also began ploughing geometrically, instead of making furrows parallel to the contours of slope, which exacerbated erosion caused by surface runoff. The heavy machinery also compacted the soil much more than horses did, which depleted its moisture-holding capacity and reduced the rooting depth of crops, leading to more erosion. Finally, eliminating draught animals from modern farming practices also eliminated their manure, a natural and convenient source of fertilizer, and forced farmers to become reliant on chemical fertilizers.

Dependency on chemical fertilizers increased during the 1950s. Inorganic nitrogenous fertilizer became available at cheap prices as the explosives industries tried to establish new markets after the Second World War. Farmers began applying large quantities of fertilizers to compensate for the loss of soil fertility caused by soil erosion. This too had implications. Adding nitrogenous fertilizer reduces the organic matter in soil by stimulating decomposition. This in turn changes the physical properties of the soil that influence moisture-holding capacity, compaction and vulnerability to erosion. The result: soil with less water-holding capacity and thus less ability to absorb rainfall. This creates more runoff and accelerates erosion. Modern farmers fell into a vicious cycle of adding fertilizer to compensate for soil erosion caused by heavy equipment, which only increased the rate of soil erosion and made them even more dependent on chemical fertilizers.

Animal husbandry techniques also changed. In the past, animals spent most of their lives in the fields and were confined only intermittently for milking or shearing. Today, animal production occurs in highly controlled and contained environments such as feedlots, dairies, swine operations and poultry houses. This increases productivity and gives the farmer much more control over variables such as climate and diet, but creates very concentrated volumes of animal wastes that could run off into surface-water or seep into ground-water unless they are treated and stored properly.

At the same time, farmers have become highly specialized. Instead of growing a variety of crops and raising a variety of animals, most focus on producing a single crop or raising a single species of animal. This shift means animal production has been largely divorced from crop production, making it more difficult to follow the traditional practice of using animal wastes as manure to grow crops. In effect, manure has changed from being an essential source of nutrients to a waste product that must be disposed of.

While concentrated animal production creates problems, single crop production has also proved damaging. Monocultures encourage pests, increasing the farmer's dependence on pesticides. The high nitrogen content in fertilized crop plants also favours pests, forcing farmers to rely on chemical pesticides. But by applying pesticides, farmers destroy natural pest controls – beneficial insects, birds and other vertebrates – thus increasing their dependence on insecticides.

Finally, the agroindustry developed and successfully marketed new, high yield crop varieties. In order to realize these high yields, however, farmers had to provide the crops with near-optimal conditions for success, namely, large quantities of pesticides and fertilizers. Agriculture is now the biggest source of non-point pollution in most countries. In the US, runoff from agricultural activities is the leading source of water quality contamination in streams and lakes, and in England and Wales, farms account for 13 per cent of all substantiated water pollution incidents. There are four main problems associated with agricultural runoff: nutrients, pesticides, animal wastes and erosion.

Nutrients

Fertilizers are applied in large volumes, and not all is incorporated by the crop.

On average, plants take up only 30–50 per cent of the nitrogen, 7–15 per cent of the phosphorus and 30–50 per cent of the potash (see Table 3.1). What happens to the remainder? Some of it disperses into the atmosphere, some becomes stored in the soil on-site, and some moves off-site, either by being carried in runoff to surface-water, or by leaching down through the soil and eventually into ground-water.

As discussed in Chapter 1, too many nutrients in surface-water cause eutrophication and oxygen depletion. Nitrate levels have

Table 3.1 *Projected Fate of Agricultural Chemicals*

Media (per cent)	Pesticides	Nitrogen	Phosphorus
Atmosphere	30–50 **	15 **	<5 ***
On-site storage/decay	20–65 **	10–30 *	55–75 **
Plant uptake	4–20 ***	35–50 *	7–15 *
Off-site soil (surface)	1–10 ***	5–10 ***	10–15 ***
Surface-water	1–5 *	<5 *	5–10 *
Soil below root zone/ ground-water	<5 *	5–15 **	<1 **

* generally accurate, ** somewhat accurate, *** best guesstimate.
Source: Waddell and Bower (1988)

been increasing in many lakes and rivers in recent years, due mainly to a steady increase in the use of nitrogen fertilizers. In countries where intensive agriculture is practised, agricultural runoff contributes roughly two-thirds of nitrogen loads and one-third of phosphorus loads in the aquatic environment.

Nitrogen

Nitrogen comes in several forms: organic nitrogen, which is associated with soil particles, gaseous nitrogen, and soluble nitrates, nitrites and ammonia. The soluble forms are prone to dissolving in surface runoff. Organic nitrogen can also be carried in runoff attached to soil particles. Because nitrates are negatively charged, they are most likely to leach into ground-water. Nitrate leaching is maximized in coarse-textured soils and in soils with large continuous pores, such as those under minimum or reduced tillage. A study in California (Singh and Sekhon, 1978–9) found it takes 10 years, on average, for nitrates to percolate from the soil surface to a depth of 15 metres.

Table 3.2 *Nitrogen from Fertilizer per Square Kilometre of Agricultural Land, 1990*

Canada	1.7	Iceland	0.7
United States	2.4	Ireland	6.6
Japan	11.7	Italy	5.1
Australia	0.1	The Netherlands	19.5
New Zealand	0.3	Norway	11.4
Austria	3.9	Portugal	3.7
Belgium/Luxembourg	12.4	Spain	3.5
Denmark	14.2	Sweden	6.2
Finland	7.7	Switzerland	3.6
France	8.1	Turkey	3.3
Germany	9.9	UK	8.8
Greece	4.7		

Source: OECD (1994)

PHOSPHORUS

Phosphorus compounds are continually undergoing complex transformations in the environment: adsorption and precipitation reactions; microbial decomposition; mineralization of organic phosphorus to inorganic phosphorus; and plant uptake of inorganic phosphorus. Runoff can carry this phosphorus to surface-water bodies, where it causes eutrophication. The predominant reactions that occur following applications of phosphorus fertilizers to soils are those with aluminium, iron or calcium ions in the soil to form insoluble precipitates. These complex adsorption and precipitation reactions also mean that phosphorus moves very slowly through the soil, so it is not generally considered a threat to ground-water. However, in areas with soils with a high organic content overlying high water tables, phosphorus leaching may become significant.

Pesticides

Another cornerstone of intensive agriculture is the use of pesticides. These are a group of chemicals used to kill unwanted insects, weeds, nematodes and fungi. In 1948, the Swiss chemist Paul Muller was awarded the Nobel Prize for his discovery of the insecticidal properties of DDT. His discovery marked the beginning of an era of ever-increasing pesticide use. In the US, for example, pesticide use in agriculture nearly tripled between 1965 and 1985. Today, 45,000 pesticide products are sold in the US each year, totalling over 0.55 billion kilograms.

Most pesticides are non-specific, meaning they kill much more than the particular organisms they are used to control. Higher species can be affected, such as birds, fish and humans. In 1962, Rachel Carson published *Silent Spring*, and exposed some of the dangers of pesticides, in particular the decimation of songbirds caused by DDT. More recently, research has linked pesticides to various disorders in humans, including cancer, hormone disruption and immune disfunction.

The original long-lived, chlorinated, hydrocarbon-based insecticides such as DDT have now been largely replaced with short-lived

Table 3.3 *Consumption of Pesticides per Square Kilometre of Arable Land, 1990*

Canada	81	Italy	760
US	199	The Netherlands	1995
Japan	1807	Norway	137
Denmark	186	Sweden	83
Finland	81	Switzerland	412
France	451	Turkey	122
Germany	463	UK	371
Ireland	185		

Source: OECD (1994)

chemicals (see Table 3.4). These include organophosphates such as malathion and carbamates such as aldicarb that work by attacking the nervous system. These newer pesticides are not prone to bioconcentration, so they avoid some of the problems of DDT, but they are more acutely lethal.

There are many different classes of herbicides (see Table 3.5), with different modes of action. Triazines are made up of carbon and nitrogen atoms that form a six-sided ring. They tend to be relatively water soluble compared with other herbicides and are therefore most likely to cause surface-water or ground-water contamination. Substituted ureas work by blocking photosynthesis, while substituted anilines interfere with plant enzymes and inhibit root or shoot growth. Phenoxy herbicides actually mimic natural plant growth regulators and kill weeds by forcing them to grow too quickly.

After a pesticide is applied to a field, it may meet with a variety of fates. Only 4–20 per cent of the pesticides applied is taken up by crops. The remainder may be lost to the atmosphere through volatilization, carried away to surface-waters by runoff and erosion, or degraded by sunlight. Pesticides can also be transformed by soil organisms into other chemical forms, or leached downward with water below the crop root zone. One of the biggest problems associated with pesticide use is pollution caused by runoff. The overall mean of surface runoff discharges for all classes of pesti-

Table 3.4 *Common Insecticides*

Organochlorines	Organophosphates	Carbamates
Dicofol	Acephate	Aldicarb
Dieldrin	Chlorpyrifos	Bendicarb
Lindane	Diazinon	Carbaryl
Methoxychlor	Malathion	
	Methyl parathion	

cides is 1.2 per cent of the total pesticides applied, but if there is a big rainfall after pesticides have been applied to a field, local streams and rivers can be hit with an intense dose. US Geological Survey figures (cited in Southe and Piper, 1992) show triazines in 50 per cent of streams prior to spring field applications and 90 per cent after spring applications; of these, 34 per cent exceeded Environmental Protection Agency (EPA) drinking-water standards for the herbicide alachlor. Another problem is pesticides leaching into ground-water. Little is known about the dissipation of pesticides below the root zone. Until recent years, scientists assumed

Table 3.5 *Common Herbicides*

Triazines	Substituted amides
Atrazine	Alachlor
Cyanazine	
Simazine	
Phenoxy herbicides	Substituted ureas
2,4D	Diuron
Dicamba	Fenuron
MCPA	
Mecoprop	
Carbamates	Pyridines
Chlorpropham	Paraquat
Substituted anilines	Amino acids
Trifluralin	Glyphosate

that pesticides generally would not leach to ground-water. It was thought that most of the pesticides would either degrade quickly or remain essentially at the soil surface, attached to soil particles or organic matter. However, preliminary data indicate that a proportion of pesticides reaching the soil does leach below the root zone. This is particularly likely in soils that are sandy, low in organic matter or located in some karst regions.

Two properties determine whether a pesticide represents a threat to ground-water: its persistence and its mobility in soil. Persistence depends on how readily a pesticide can be broken down into harmless metabolites. Generally, the more similar a chemical compound is to a natural microbial metabolite, the more likely it is to be easily degraded and therefore the less likely it is to percolate into ground-water. Two factors affect a pesticide's mobility: its organic carbon sorption coeffecent, that is, the likelihood that it will bind to the surface of soil particles, and its half-life (see Table 3.4). A pesticide with a small organic carbon sorption coefficient and long half-life poses a considerable threat to ground-water through leaching, particularly in soils with little organic matter. A pesticide with a large organic carbon sorption coefficient and a long half-life is more likely to remain on or near the surface of soils with moderate levels of organic carbon content, thereby increasing its chances of being carried to a lake or stream in runoff. In terms of water quality protection, pesticides with intermediate sorption coefficients and short half-lives may be considered 'safest'. Although they are not readily

Table 3.6 *Relative Mobility of Selected Pesticides in Soil-Water Systems*

Moderately or very mobile
Dicamba, MCPA, 2,4D, simazine

Slightly mobile
Atrazine, alachlor, cyanazine, diuron

Nearly or completely immobile
Diazinon, lindane, methyl parathion, parathion, dieldrin, trifluralin, DDT

Source: Waddell and Blair, 1988

leached, they move into the soil with water, thereby reducing their potential for loss from erosion, and they degrade fairly rapidly, thereby reducing the chance for losses below the root zone.

Animal Wastes

Although fertilizers and pesticides are the biggest forms of agricultural pollution, there are others. Farm slurry and silage effluent are responsible for serious incidents of local pollution. Livestock manure, for example, is the principal non-point source of nutrient pollution in Canada. Farm slurry is a semi-liquid mix of animal waste products that is 100 times more concentrated than raw sewage. There's lots of it – cattle alone produce 40 kilograms or more of manure for every kilogram of edible beef that is eventually marketed. Silage effluent, created when stored grass is fermented in the absence of air, is up to 200 times as polluting as raw sewage. Normally these wastes are spread on agricultural land or treated in lagoons, but when accidents or carelessness occur, they can cause serious pollution.

Like sewage, animal wastes have a high BOD, and contain suspended solids, nitrates, phosphorus and faecal coliform bacteria. Untreated, they can cause eutrophication in surface-water, as well as increasing turbidity. Water contaminated with animal wastes can also transmit diseases: serious outbreaks of cryptosporidium in the UK caused by contaminated drinking-water have been traced to spores in the faeces of infected cattle grazing upstream from water treatment plants.

Soil Erosion

Finally, there is soil erosion. Anywhere there is bare soil, wind and water can carry off organic material and fine clay mineral particles from the soil and deposit them in local waterways. Tilling fields also encourages erosion. In many areas, soil erosion is reaching crisis proportions – most US farms, for example, lose at least 5 tonnes of soil per hectare per year. In fact, erosion from cropland is the single largest source of non-point pollution in the US and represents 50 per cent of suspended solid pollution. In 1977 the US Soil Conservation Service initiated a National Resource Inventory to document how much soil was blowing and washing away. The finding was 9 tonnes per hectare, almost twice the 'officially tolerable' average annual replacement rate of 5 tonnes per hectare. The inventory was repeated in 1982. This time the average loss from croplands was 18 tonnes per hectare.

Chapter 4

Case-Studies: The Rhine and the Great Lakes

I've chosen two case-studies to illustrate the complex nature of water pollution: the Great Lakes in North America and the Rhine in Europe. Both bodies of water fall under the jurisdiction of several different governments; both suffer from a range of pollution problems; both are used for a number of different (and often opposing) purposes; and both are the subject of international clean-up efforts. They share some important similarities and offer some interesting contrasts.

Introduction

THE RHINE

The head-waters of the Rhine are in east central Switzerland. From there, the river flows for 1320 kilometres through Germany, France, the Netherlands and Luxembourg before it reaches the North Sea (see Figure 4.1). Its catchment area covers 190,000 square kilometres and is home to 50 million people. It serves as a major artery for western Europe: at the mouth of the Rhine, Rotterdam is the world's largest seaport, while upstream, Duisburg is the world's largest inland port. The Rhine valley, particularly in Germany, is heavily industrialized: 20 per cent of the world's chemicals are produced here. It is also a very intensively farmed area, particularly in the Netherlands, where crop yields and agrochemical inputs are among the highest in the world. These uses are often at odds with

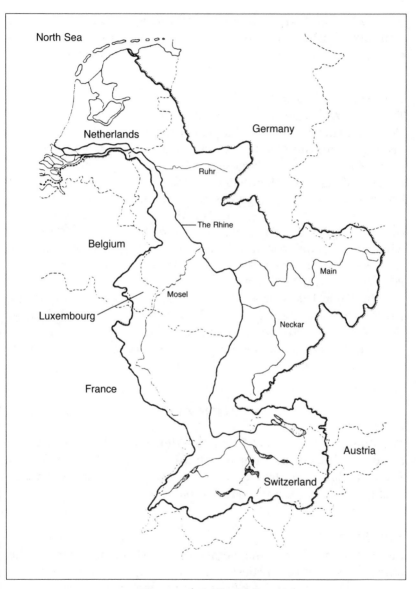

Figure 4.1 *The Rhine*

each other and are the source of international conflict. For example, the Netherlands needs clean water for irrigation, but receives water polluted by French mines and German industry.

THE GREAT LAKES

The North American Great Lakes comprise five lakes, Ontario, Erie, Michigan, Huron and Superior, which drain out of the St Lawrence River and into the Atlantic Ocean (see Figure 4.2). Together they represent the world's largest freshwater ecosystem. The Great Lakes basin is more than 520,000 square kilometres in area, and home to 8.5 million Canadians and 32.5 million Americans. This vast area falls under several jurisdictions: the US–Canada border runs through four of the five lakes and their connecting rivers, while at the state/provincial level, they are variously governed by Ontario, Minnesota, Wisconsin, Illinois, Michigan, Ohio, Pennsylvania and New York.

The Great Lakes support the largest freshwater fishery in the world. They are a source of drinking-water and hydroelectricity; the site of industrial, commercial, agricultural and urban development; and a conduit for shipping; and they are used for a variety of recreational purposes.

History

The Rhine and the Great Lakes experienced peak levels of water pollution during the industrial boom of the 1940s, 1950s and 1960s. Pollution control legislation subsequently improved water quality, but in both cases major problems remain.

THE RHINE

In 1979, a member of the Netherlands parliament described the Rhine as 'surely the dirtiest water in Europe'. The roots of the problem can be traced back hundreds of years. Major organic pollution began when the cities along the river constructed sewerage systems for municipal waste and industries began to discharge waste-water directly into the river. As the cities grew bigger, and as

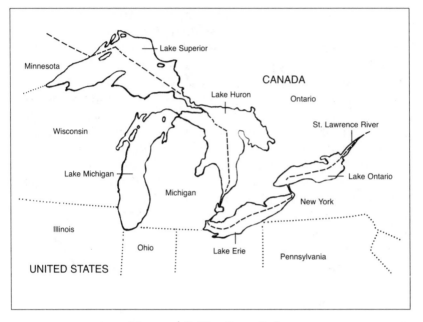

Figure 4.2 *The Great Lakes*

agriculture became more intensive, the levels of nutrients increased. Concurrently, increasing industrialization created more heavy metal waste and organic micropollutants, and an increase in inland water shipping brought greater risk of spills.

Water pollution has been a serious problem for many years: there have been reports of lifeless zones downstream from major cities since the beginning of the century. In the decades after the Second World War, the quality of water in the Rhine got progressively worse. The economic resurgence in central Europe in the 1960s and early 1970s created water pollution levels high enough to wipe out dozens of species of fish and other creatures. Most of the river became unsuitable for swimming, and the production of drinking-water was threatened. In the summer of 1971, peak levels of pollution made a stretch of more than 100 kilometres completely oxygenless.

The turnaround came in the mid 1970s, when improvements were made on several fronts. Pollution from point sources decreased for four reasons. The primary reason was the construction of sewage treatment plants: between 1973 and 1981, the percentage of sewage treated rose from 30 per cent to over 80 per cent. This, coupled with the use of phosphate-free detergents, steadily reduced phosphorus levels in the river. In addition, industrial 'good housekeeping' practices were instituted: there were substantial increases in recycling of industrial sludges and solid wastes by metal-producing industries, and cleaner industrial processes replaced older technologies. Metal and synthetic organic chemical pollution declined. There were also reductions in pollution from diffuse sources: the reduction in acid rain meant less corrosion of zinc from galvanized steel and therefore less zinc pollution, while atmospheric deposition of lead, cadmium and zinc also declined substantially from the mid 1960s onwards. These improvements culminated in 1992, in the return of sexually mature salmon to the Rhine. However, as Table 4.1 indicates, there has been a net degradation in the Rhine over the course of the century.

THE GREAT LAKES

The degradation of the Great Lakes began with European settlement. The newcomers cleared mature forests, removing protective shade, and then constructed sawmills that clogged the streams with sawdust. The cleared areas were farmed, causing erosion that further clogged the streams, and fish were harvested indiscriminately. Next came industrialization and urbanization. Pollution reached a peak in the decades following the Second World War: industrial wastes turned Michigan's Rouge River orange, while the Cuyahoga River in Ohio was so clogged with grease and oils that it repeatedly caught on fire. The river had to be declared a fire hazard, and protective walls were built on either side. One of the most infamous cases of contamination was at Love Canal, a suburb in New York State not far from Niagara Falls. The story began in the 1940s when Hooker (now Occidental Chemical Corporation) bought an abandoned canal and used it as a chemical disposal site. Over a decade, nearly 20,000 tonnes of chemical waste were dumped in the canal. The city of Niagara Falls bought the land from Hooker and built residential homes and an elementary school on the site. But hazardous chemicals leaked from the canal, causing high rates of miscarriage, birth

Table 4.1 *Changes in Species Richness of Macroinvertebrates*

| | Upper Rhine | | Middle Rhine | | Lower Rhine | |
	1916	1980	1916	1980	1900s	1980s
Snails	8	4	8	5	11	10
Mussels	11	4	10	4	14	7
Crustaceans	3	2	3	2	14	7
Beetles	2	1	1	0	1	1
Dragon-flies	2	1	1	0	3	2
May-flies	11	4	3	0	21	2
Stone-flies	13	0	12	0	13	0
Caddis-flies	11	5	11	2	17	5

defects and other reproductive problems. Eventually thousands of people were evacuated from the site, and Love Canal was declared a national emergency area in 1978.

According to Janet Abramovitz, 'attempts to heal the Great Lakes have been limited largely to episodes of crisis management' (Brown et al, 1996). These began early in the century when typhoid and cholera epidemics, caused by drinking-water contaminated with sewage, killed thousands. The short-sighted solution chosen by the municipal authorities was to extend sewage outfall pipes further into the lakes, away from the drinking-water intakes. Later in the century, eutrophication became an extremely serious problem. In the 1960s, Lake Erie was filled with blue–green algae, dead fish floated on the surface and beaches were covered with rotting masses of *Cladophora* algae. Oxygen levels plummeted, aquatic species were rapidly becoming extinct, and some scientists declared the lake was ecologically 'dead'. This crisis provided the impetus to regulate phosphate emissions, and the US and Canada jointly agreed to control municipal and industrial waste-water emissions. Phosphorus levels subsequently decreased. Phosphate regulations were followed by a US–Canada agreement in the early 1970s to restrict the use of organochlorine pesticides, PCBs and mercury. This successfully reduced organic chemical and heavy metal pollution in the Great Lakes. Despite these important gains, pollution control management has tended to focus on 'end of pipe' management of individual chemicals, rather than on comprehensive source reductions.

Current Levels of Pollution

The countries bordering the Rhine have formed an international commission to tackle the issue of water pollution, as have Canada and the US. As a result, big improvements have been made to water quality, but problems remain. Both commissions have compiled lists of priority pollutants contaminating their respective bodies of water. There is significant overlap: mercury, PCBs, aldrin, dieldrin, DDT and hexachlorobenzene are problems in both areas. Non-point source pollution is also a serious issue.

THE RHINE

The Rhine is heavily used, both as a source of water and as a receptacle for waste-water. More than 20 per cent of the average flow is used as drinking-water or as industrial rinsing and cooling water – uses that require high quality water. At the same time, the Rhine has to cope with high pollution loads, particularly of metals, salts and nitrates.

The metal issue has been tackled most successfully, and metal pollution has declined by more than 90 per cent in the past two decades. This is attributable to a number of things. The shift to unleaded petrol has reduced lead pollution considerably. The construction of large numbers of sewage treatment plants in the late 1960s and 1970s helped to reduce the levels of nickel, zinc and chromium, as have stricter industrial regulations encouraging the use of closed loop cycles, where metals are reused. Metal contamination remains a problem in a few spots, such as the sediments in the port of Rotterdam.

Salt pollution continues to be a difficult problem. Although the natural chloride content of the Rhine is 10 milligrams per litre; salt concentrations can reach almost 600 milligrams per litre at the Germany–Netherlands border, and international agreements have done little to reduce this. The biggest sources of salt pollution are the French potash mines in Alsace. Unfortunately, there is no inexpensive way to remove salts; the current strategy is to desalinate water only when it is absolutely necessary for irrigation.

Progress on nitrogen pollution has been mixed. While ammonia levels have dropped in the past 20 years, nitrate levels have actually risen, mainly because of heavy fertilizer use. The result is eutrophication. In the slow-moving Dutch waters, in the German Bight and near the Danish coast, algae are clogging the waterways and causing oxygen depletion. In an attempt to tackle the nitrate issue, the European Union gives subsidies to farmers who take land out of cultivation, while Germany subsidizes farmers who avoid using fertilizers near the banks of the Rhine.

On the toxic chemical front, the International Commission for the Protection of the Rhine against Pollution has categorized the following substances as 'List I ' (priority) pollutants:

- mercury and all mercury compounds
- cadmium and all cadmium compounds
- dieldrin
- endrin
- aldrin
- chlordane
- heptachlor
- heptachloroexpoxide
- hexachlorobenzene
- hexachlorocyclohexane
- polychlorobiphenyl compounds
- DDT
- pentachlorophenol
- hexachlorobutadiene
- endosulfan

Flooding is also a problem. In the upper reaches, the Rhine has been cut off from 90 per cent of its orginal floodplain by embankments, reservoirs and channelization. As a result, the river flows much faster and with more force than it would naturally, causing flooding in the downstream areas. In 1982, Germany and France agreed to create flood meadows upstream to alleviate these problems, but progress has been slow, with only two of the 20 designated areas having been completed. In the lower reaches, the Netherlands has begun to restore some of the floodplain, with the ultimate goal of converting 15 per cent of farmland back to floodplain.

Finally, there is an ongoing danger of spills. On a heavily industrialized, heavily trafficked waterway, accidents are inevitable. An infamous example occurred on 1 November, 1986, when a Swiss warehouse full of pesticides caught fire near Basel. The water sprayed on the fire washed 10,000 tonnes of toxic chemicals into the river, killing thousands of fish, eels and macroinvertebrates for several hundred kilometres downstream. Remarkably, the river fauna recovered within 2 years, although the ground-water in the Rhine alluvial aquifer remains polluted.

THE GREAT LAKES

Although stricter regulations have reduced the amount of pollution entering the lakes, the pollution created in previous years is still a problem. Only 1 per cent of the water in the system flows out each year, so toxics stick around for a long time, both in the water and in the bottom sediments. Today the major pollution sources in the Great Lakes are industrial chemicals, household hazardous waste, airborne pollutants, runoff and spills.

Persistent organic chemicals and metals are two of the biggest problems facing the Great Lakes. These toxins accumulate in body tissues, so a fish, for example, concentrates more and more toxins in its body the longer it stays in the Great Lakes. Furthermore, the toxins become magnified through the food chain: a big fish that feeds on little fish will ingest the toxins accumulated in the little fish, magnifying the amount in its tissues, and the bird that eats the big fish will ingest even more (see Table 4.2). The higher a species is in the food chain, the bigger the risk. Particularly disturbing is the fact that several organic chemicals actually mimic hormones, interfering with reproductive systems and immune systems.

In the early 1970s, water-birds in the Great Lakes were among the most heavily contaminated in the world. Today the situation has improved, but tumours, birth defects and reproductive

Table 4.2 *Bioconcentration of PCBs in Lake Ontario's Ecosystem (Parts per Trillion)*

Lake-water	50
Spottail shiners	200,000
Bottom dwellers	1,300,000
Rainbow smelt	900,000
Coho salmon	4,200,000
Lake trout	6,400,000
Herring gull egg	40,000,000

problems still plague several species of fish. Many long-lived, fish-eating species in the Great Lakes basin also remain affected by toxic chemicals. Birth defects have been recorded in ten species of young fish-eating birds in the basin; the prevalence of crossed bills in cormorant chicks in Green Bay, Lake Michigan, is 22–87 times higher than normal. As the Royal Commission of the Future of Toronto's Waterfront aptly points out, 'Our water quality standards are not set to protect the gull that eats the smelt, or the human who eats the trout that ate the smelt'. Herring gulls have been selected as indicators of lake-wide contamination because they prey predominantly on fish and they remain in the basin all year round. Overall, they exhibit poor health, reproductive problems and decreased population size. In the early 1970s, PCB concentrations in herring gull eggs were millions of times the levels detectable in water. Following the regulations on the use of organochloride pesticides in the 1960s and 1970s, and the voluntary reduction in the production of PCBs in 1971, the concentration of contaminants in herring gulls has decreased greatly. However, wildlife continues to feel the effects of pollution. The most dramatic and disturbing example is that of the beluga whales. These mammals live in the St Lawrence River, which drains the Great Lakes. They are one of the most contaminated animals on earth, laden with DDT, PCBs and heavy metals and ridden with cancers. When they die, the corpses are legally classified as hazardous waste.

The limited studies on human health suggest that the general population in the Great Lakes basin is probably not exposed to higher levels of critical pollutants than other North American populations. However, some specific subgroups who consume large amounts of fish or wildlife, particularly Native Americans, have higher than average levels of several persistent chemical contaminants that have been linked to problems in child development. The International Joint Commission has identified 11 critical pollutants in the Great Lakes based on their presence, degree of toxicity, persistence and ability to bioconcentrate and bioaccumulate. All 11 are widely distributed; they include industrial chemicals, pesticides and waste byproducts. Currently, despite some regulatory controls, they persist at levels that exceed the guidelines in some areas of the ecosystem. They are as follows:

- PCBs
- mercury
- alkylated lead
- aldrin
- dieldrin
- DDT and its metabolites
- toxaphene
- mirex
- hexachlorobenzene
- benzo(a)pyrene
- furans
- dioxins

Other types of pollution are also problematic. The Great Lakes are particularly vulnerable to air pollution because of their large surface area: airborne pollutants from as far away as Mexico contaminate them. Runoff, both from urban areas and from agriculture, is an increasing problem. Finally, aquatic communites are stressed by exotic species, overfishing and excess fish stocking; degradation and loss of tributary and near-shore habitat; the impact of persistent toxic chemicals; and localized eutrophication.

Legislation

Many freshwater resources in the world are shared by two or more nations. Some of the oldest international treaties and organizations were created to regulate the use of shared water bodies, including the Rhine and the Great Lakes. Water pollution agreements grew out of general agreements on water use. In both the Rhine and the Great Lakes, they have met with only limited success.

THE RHINE

Transboundary management of the Rhine began in 1869, when the Central Commission for Rhine Shipping was established to create an international forum for shipping problems. However, it was not until the next century that pollution became an international issue. In 1950, the International Rhine Commission began studying waste-water and water quality problems. In 1953, Switzerland, France, Luxembourg, Germany and the Netherlands formed the International Commission for the Protection of the Rhine against Pollution (IKSR). Its purpose was to coordinate multinational efforts and to monitor levels of contaminants in the river.

Much of the early work of the IKSR focussed exclusively on the salt issue. Salt pollution has been a long-standing issue in the Rhine – as early as 1932, the Dutch government protested against French salt emissions. In 1976, the IKSR passed the Convention on the Protection of the Rhine against Chloride Pollution. Unfortunately, the chloride treaty led to only small reductions in salt discharges by France. In the 1960s, the IKSR turned to the problems of cooling-water, eutrophication and heavy metals, and in 1976 it passed the Convention on the Protection of the Rhine against Chemical Pollution.

The IKSR serves as a useful venue for exchanging information about national pollution abatement techniques. It monitors pollution and issues an annual report with extensive analytical data. It also serves as a centre for cooperation in research and coordination of warnings in case of spills. But it has weaknesses: one of the biggest criticisms of IKSR is that it cannot create binding rules; it can only make recommendations to national governments.

In 1986, the Rhine Action Programme was launched by Switzerland, Germany, France, the Netherlands and Luxembourg. It has four objectives: long-term safeguarding of drinking-water; decontamination of sediments; re-establishment of higher species of fish; and protection of the North Sea. The programme signified an important change, as for the first time an ecological objective was formulated for the whole river, and the measures to be taken were related to this objective. The results have been positive. In 1989, an inventory was compiled of all discharges of 30 different hazardous substances. By 1995, the rates of discharge for all 30 had been reduced by 50 per cent or more. Improved safeguards have prevented or limited discharges to the river after accidental spills, and fish ladders help salmon get upstream to spawning grounds.

THE GREAT LAKES

The Boundary Waters Treaty was created in 1909 to address issues concerning the Great Lakes and other waters that lay on the boundary between the US and Canada. One of these issues was pollution: according to the treaty, 'waters flowing across the boundary shall not be polluted on either side to the injury of health or property of the other' (1909 Boundary Waters Treaty, cited in Cooper, 1986). The treaty established the International Joint Commission (IJC), a quasi-judicial body with the power to give or refuse approval for the use, obstruction or diversion of boundary waters. The first bilateral environmental initiative was undertaken in 1912, when the Canadian and US governments asked the IJC to study sewage issues. Sixty years later, the first Great Lakes Water Quality Agreement (GLWQA) was established, largely in response to the critical state of Lake Erie. The 1972 GLWQA focussed mainly on eutrophication problems in Lake Erie and Lake Ontario. It set effluent targets for sewage treatment plants and established a schedule for reducing phosphorus discharges into the lakes. Since 1972, the GLWQA has been amended twice. In 1978, the Agreement was modified to place more emphasis on persistent industrial pollutants and toxic chemicals, establishing water quality objectives for specific chemicals. It also contained two dramatic new initiatives. One was the goal of zero discharge of persistent toxic substances. 'There is no acceptable assimilative capacity for persistent, bioaccumulative toxic substances', the IJC declared. The other was a proposal to use an ecosystem approach to protect the environment.

In 1985, the IJC came out with a list of 11 pollutants of greatest concern, based on their persistence in the environment, toxicity to wildlife, and possible human health effects.

The 1987 revisions to the GLWQA took a broader view of pollution entering the Great Lakes. It created new annexes to address pollution from airborne toxics, contaminated sediments and ground-water, and pollution from urban and agricultural runoff. It also committed Canadians and Americans to develop Remedial Action Plans for 42 severely polluted sites. One of the features of these Remedial Action Plans was that they called for public involvement in the regulatory process: public committees were established to advise teams of technical experts on the task of cleaning up local polluted sites.

The Future

THE RHINE

The Rhine Action Programme has been criticized for not going far enough. There are several barriers that prevent its final objectives from being met. Pollution must be reduced much further than the 50 per cent agreed to in the programme. Diffuse sources must be tackled, particularly agriculture and air pollution. Finally, the habitat of the river must be restored, including its tributaries and floodplains. The complexity of current problems calls for a shift to integrated pollution control encompassing all sources of pollution affecting the Rhine. It also requires an international body with real powers that are fully supported by national governments.

THE GREAT LAKES

Unlike the Rhine Action Programme, the Great Lake agreements, by and large, are stringent enough to protect the environment. The problem lies in implementation and enforcement. Because the agreements do not have the force of law, they rely on public pressure and political will among the member jurisdictions to achieve their goals. According to a citizen's review of the GLWQA (GLWUQTF, 1987), federal, provincial and state governments have failed to implement the GLWQA, and, in some instances, have not even enforced their own existing laws and regulations. Furthermore, the current climate of cutbacks to research, education and enforcement programmes in Ontario and several US states threatens to undo much of the progress that has been made in the past two decades.

Part II

Prevention

Chapter 5

Prevention

Prevention, as the saying goes, is nine-tenths of the cure. This is simplistic, but true. Preventing water pollution is much easier, cheaper and more effective than trying to undo the damage it does. The more we minimize pollution, the less we have to clean up. Unfortunately, this has not been the traditional approach.

Throughout the early years of the century, environmental protection focussed on local, clearly visible problems caused by industrial or municipal discharge. Scientists believed that we could rely on the assimilative capacity of receiving waters to deal with pollution, so long as this capacity was not overwhelmed. Thus, dilution was the most common approach. Next came 'end of pipe' solutions. This approach also tackled very localized pollution sources, for example, building waste-water treatment plants to clean a city's municipal sewage before discharging it into the local river. Often these treatment systems were established only when pollution reached crisis proportions, for example, in response to typhoid epidemics. Finally, a growing environmental awareness in the mid 1980s led to the adoption of pollution prevention, generally defined as 'the use of processes, practices, materials and energy that avoid or minimize the creation of pollutants and wastes' (Government of Canada, 1995). In 1990, the passing of the US Pollution Prevention Act gave top priority to pollution prevention whenever feasible, declaring it is 'fundamentally different and more desirable than waste management and pollution control'. The Act established a national policy of hierarchical environmental protection, ranking pollution prevention above recycling, treatment and disposal. One of the reasons for favouring pollution prevention over 'end of pipe' solutions is that the latter are not terribly feasible for pollution that does not come from a single, definable source: non-point pollution, such as runoff from agriculture, forestry and construction; urban runoff; and atmospheric deposition.

Until recently, the focus of water pollution control has been on treating point sources. Governments created regulations to govern discharges from municipal sewage treatment plants and industrial outfalls. However, as regulations on point source pollution became stricter, non-point sources became responsible for an increasing proportion of total water pollution (see Table 5.1). According to the US 1990 National Water Quality Inventory, non-point pollutants were the most commonly reported contaminants in the nation's water bodies.

By its nature, prevention is highly specific to the type and source of pollution. The rest of this chapter presents some examples of pollution prevention, grouped under the headings used in the first section of the book: urbanization, industrialization and intensive agriculture.

Table 5.1 *Sources of Pollution Causing Impairment of US Surface-waters*

Source	Rivers	Lakes
Non-point pollution	65	75
Other	18	8
Industrial point sources	9	7
Sewage treatment plants	2	3

Source: EPA (1989) cited in Olson (1993)

Urbanization

ECOSYSTEM RESTORATION

The less vulnerable an ecosystem is to pollution, the less damage pollution will do. Yet many urban ecosystems have been seriously weakened and degraded. Restoration projects can help to strengthen ecosystems, by increasing their capacity to absorb and assimilate pollution. Urban river restoration offers an excellent example of this.

Table 5.2 Water Quality Impairment by Non-point Pollutants

Source	Rivers	Lakes
Agricultural runoff	41	23
Unknown	26	37
Natural	8	10
Mining	8	7
Hydromodification	6	6
Urban runoff	4	6
Land disposal	3	4
Construction	2	2

Source: EPA (1986, 1990) cited in Olson and Smoley (1993)

Major river works have been carried out in almost all European countries and across North America to facilitate navigation, to control floods, to produce hydroelectricity or to improve drainage of adjacent farmland. Often the path of the river is changed and the banks are channelized, resulting in less habitat diversity, a reduced ability to cope with pollution and a greater variation in flow rates. Ravines may be filled in and tributaries may be converted into underground sewers. Housing subdivisions are built on floodplains, while wetlands are drained to create more land, eliminate mosquito breeding grounds or improve access to ports and harbours. Yet natural features such as forested banks, intact floodplains and ample wetlands are essential to the proper functioning of a river. Undisturbed floodplains filter out sediments and nutrients before they reach the river, thus improving water quality. Wetlands control flooding, absorb pollutants, release purified water to ground-water and streams and provide havens for wildlife. Woodlands recharge ground-water as well as create wildlife habitats. When these features are destroyed, the natural interactions between the river and its floodplain are disrupted, the river is less able to cope with pollution and the likelihood of flooding is increased.

Local planning departments play a key role in protecting and restoring local waterways. By prohibiting construction on sensitive land and floodplains, and preserving woodlands and wetlands, planning departments can increase the resistance of aquatic ecosys-

---

> ## *Box 5.1 The Task Force to Bring Back the Don*
>
> The Task Force to Bring Back the Don is a group of citizens working to restore Toronto's Don River. They offer the following suggestions for restoration:
>
> - plant trees in the watershed to slow water percolation through the soil and create a more stable water flow in the river
> - prevent erosion by placing rocks along stream banks
> - plant native trees and shrubs to stabilize stream beds
> - create wetlands to control flooding and absorb pollutants
> - remove artificially channelled banks to slow the flow of the river
> - recreate natural deltas at the mouth of the river
> - regulate flow by creating detention areas, replacing impermeable surfaces with porous materials within the watershed, creating wetlands, constructing ditches along expressways and major roads, and reforesting
> - cluster developments on the least sensitive land while preserving river valleys, ravines, wetlands, woodlands and hillocks
>
> Source: Crombie (1992)

tems to pollution. Citizens can also take an active role in restoration: many groups have organized tree planting events or clean-up days in their local watersheds.

REDUCING AND DELAYING RUNOFF

One of the biggest issues in urban areas is storm-water, caused by paving over too much of the watershed and thus preventing rain-water from percolating into the soil. When rainstorms occur, the rain-water flows across the paved surfaces of the city, picking up a heavy load of pollutants and dumping it into local waterways in a great flood. Engineers and urban planners offer a number of suggestions for reducing and delaying runoff after rainstorms.

Many homes and buildings have drain-pipes that are connected to storm sewers. This means that when it rains, the water is funnelled directly into a storm-water collection system that empties it into local waterways. Many municipalities offer free disconnection programmes and provide rain-water collection barrels at subsidized prices. Instead of shunting the rain-water into sewers, home-owners can collect it and use it to water their lawns and gardens. This reduces pressure on the water supply system and is also better for the plants because rain-water doesn't contain the chlorine that is often present in tap-water.

On flat roofs, rooftop gardens are an excellent way to reduce storm-water and use the rain for productive purposes. The specific type of garden will depend on the load-bearing capacity of the roof. There are lots of techniques available for creating rooftop gardens with minimal weight. If the roof was not designed to be walked on, a thin layer of turf grass and wild flowers can be installed. On sturdier roofs, containers can be planted with trees, shrubs, flowers or vegetables. Special lightweight soils are available to reduce the overall load on the roof. It is also possible to locate the beds where the load-bearing capacity is greatest, along the outside edges of the roof where the structural walls will support the weight. Rooftop gardens not only reduce storm-water runoff, but also offer a number of additional advantages such as reducing heat loss duing the winter, keeping the building cooler during the summer, and even growing food for urban dwellers

Large areas of pavement contribute to urban runoff. Replacing some of this concrete and asphalt with a porous surface will allow rain-water to percolate into the underlying soil and reduce the amount of runoff. Gravel is a simple example that is suitable for private driveways. More sophisticated versions of porous pavement involve a thin layer of open-graded asphalt mix on top of a much deeper layer of crushed stone aggregate. As the storm-water trickles through the aggregate, pollutants are filtered out. Porous pavement can remove 80–100 per cent of the suspended solids, 20–70 per cent of nutrients and 15–80 per cent of the metals present in storm-water. However, porous pavement is less durable than its traditional counterpart, so it does not make good economic sense to replace all urban pavement with porous varieties. It is best suited for low traffic roads or car parks. The latter are also good candidates for vegetative buffers. These are strips of vegetation planted around the edge of the car park in order to take up some of the storm-water and filter out suspended solids, organic material and metals. Drainage ditches or infiltration trenches filled with coarse sand or gravel can also be used to delay runoff and provide a reasonable degree of treatment.

In general, the more green-space in a city, the less runoff there will be. Many cities are now creating storm-water detention ponds or wetlands to delay runoff and remove pollutants. In these systems roughly 75 per cent of suspended solids settle out, while the vegetation takes up some of the nutrients and metals. These areas often double as parks and can provide a habitat for wildlife.

EDUCATING CITIZENS

A surprising amount of urban toxic waste orginates from individual households: cleaning products, bleach, paints, solvents, lawn and garden chemicals, petrol, antifreeze and motor oil. By switching to non-toxic cleaning products, reducing or eliminating the use of lawn and garden chemicals (urban pesticide use now accounts for a significant proportion of total pesticide use), and taking hazardous wastes, such as paints, motor oils and solvents, to a hazardous waste disposal site instead of flushing them down the drain, individuals can reduce the load on sewage treatment plants and local waterways.

One example of successful public education programmes in North America is the Storm Drain Stencilling Program. Many urban residents are not aware of how the storm drain systems work, and believe that storm-water is treated at a waste-water treatment plant that will remove any contaminants present. They use the storm drains as a convenient way to dispose of used motor oils and solvents. The goals of the programme are to teach citizens that storm sewers generally flow to the nearest lake or river without any kind of treatment, and to get citizens to help reduce the amount of storm drain pollution. The programme involves training volunteers to paint some kind of symbol, such as a fish, beside street drains. Many communities have found this to be the least costly and most effective way to reduce non-point pollution.

Industrialization

ON-SITE TREATMENT

There is a growing trend in Western countries to hold industries responsible for cleaning up the pollution they create, instead of allowing industrial waste-water to be discharged to municipal sewers and taken care of by the local treatment plant. This makes good environmental sense. Municipal sewage treatment plants are not designed to remove toxic industrial wastes and metals, or even common household chemicals. Many of these chemicals can actually kill the bacteria that sewage treatment plants depend on to break down the organic matter in sewage. Furthermore, municipal sewage treatment plant operators don't know what's in the waste-water that arrives at their doorstep, because sewers contain a cocktail of mixed wastes from households and thousands of different industries. It is difficult, if not impossible, to design treatment processes to remove all the possible pollutants that might be present. The operators of individual industrial plants, on the other hand, should know exactly what their waste-water is composed of, so they can design specific treatment processes to remove the pollutants. In fact, it is often possible to reuse many of these so-called pollutants, and reduce the cost of raw materials in the process. Many jurisdictions now recognize the advantage of on-site treatment. In the US, the National Pretreatment Program makes the operators of municipal sewage treatment plants responsible for identifying which industrial users should pretreat their wastes, monitoring them to make sure they do pretreat their wastes, and enforcing the regulations if they don't comply.

SOURCE CONTROL AND WASTE MINIMIZATION

Regardless of whether treatment takes place on-site or at the municipal treatment plant, removing pollutants from waste-water is often a chemical- and energy-intensive business. Not only is this expensive, it is inherently wasteful. Raw materials are used only once and then thrown away. Instead, many companies have chosen to implement a toxics reduction programme. This could involve switching to less dangerous raw materials, or changing the production process to use these chemicals more effectively. It could mean installing a closed loop cycle, where chemicals are recovered from the waste stream and reused within the plant, or recovering waste material and selling it to another industry. For example, an increasingly common practice is to recycle organic solvents. The used solvent is distilled, producing a clean fraction that can be reused, and a residue containing the contaminants that can be incinerated.

In most cases, implementing a toxics reduction programme will actually save companies money. To return to the solvent example, reusing solvents saves money on raw materials and reduces or eliminates the cost of hazardous waste disposal. The typical payback period for the capital investment in solvent recovery equipment is less than 1 year.

As effluent regulations become stricter and the costs of incineration and landfill increase, reducing, reusing and recycling at the industrial level make economic sense. Even relatively minor changes can reduce pollution and save money: insisting on 'good housekeeping' practices, routinely checking for leaks or inefficiencies in the manufacturing process, and regularly balancing inputs and outputs to identify any unusual losses.

Box 5.2 3M's 3Ps

In 1975, 3M Corporation launched a '3P' programme: Pollution Prevention Pays. The goal was to prevent the production of pollutants at their source, rather than trying to control them at the end of the manufacturing process. The programme has four basic components: product reformulation to reduce the volume of toxic ingredients; process modification and equipment redesign to reduce wastage; and the recovery of waste materials for reuse. Employee input plays a critical role.

The programme has been an unqualified success. In the first 9 years, 1200 employee suggestions were implemented, saving almost US$200 million. It eliminated the discharge of more than 80,000 tonnes of air pollutants, 9000 tonnes of water pollutants and 130,000 tonnes of sludge. Annually, it prevented the production of roughly 40 million cubic metres of waste-water and saved 40,000 cubic metres of oil.

Instead of paying money for costly 'end of pipe' treatment to meet government discharge regulations, 3M prevents pollution, uses its raw materials more effectively and saves money.

Source: Huising *et al.* (1986)

Agriculture

TECHNIQUES FOR REDUCING SOIL EROSION

Improving Soil Fertility

At a very basic level, one of the keys to reducing soil erosion is to improve soil fertility. If crops are grown on a piece of land year after year, the soil becomes depleted. By incorporating compost or manure into the soil on a regular basis, a farmer can replace the organic material and enhance the fertility of the soil. A soil that is rich in organic material will hold water well and will be less likely to wash away in a rainstorm or blow away in the wind. For example, a 15-year experiment at Rodale Institute concludes that organic farming systems have better soil quality and less runoff than chemical farming systems (*Organic Gardening*, 1997). The study compared two sets of fields: conventional fields that grew a rotation of maize and soybeans and were treated with chemical fertilizers and herbicides, and organically maintained fields that grew a rotation of maize, soybeans, grains and hay and were mechanically weeded and fertilized with manure. Not only did the organic fields suffer less erosion, they also consistently produced the same yields as the chemically farmed fields, and comparatively higher yields during years of low rainfall. Another technique is to alternate 'heavy-feeding' crops such as maize and soybeans with soil-conserving crops such as legumes and sod-forming grasses that act as nitrogen fixers and enhance the nutrient content of the soil. A study in the state of Missouri found soil erosion rates dropped from 19.7 tons per acre per year with continuous corn cultivation to 2.7 tons per acre per year with rotation of heavy-feeding maize, less nitrogen-demanding wheat and nitrogen-fixing clover.

Following Natural Contours

Much soil erosion is caused by ploughing in straight rows instead of curves that follow the natural contours of the land. Farmers adopted straight row ploughing in the 1940s and 1950s because large farm machinery demanded it, but this meant large soil losses wherever rows lay parallel to the slope of the land. Contour ploughing on moderate slopes can reduce average soil loss by as much as 50 per cent. A related technique is contour strip cropping, where two or more crops are grown in alternating bands that follow the contours of the land. These strips are typically 15–30 metres wide and serve as buffers to catch any eroding soil. Strip cropping can reduce erosion by a further 50 per cent.

Reducing Tillage and Retaining Crop Residues
Common farming practice includes removing crop residues after the harvest. This leaves the soil bare over the winter and vulnerable to erosion. For every ton of residue that remains per acre of field, the amount of soil lost due to water erosion is reduced by 65 per cent. Alternatively, if there is little residue left after the crop has been harvested, the field can be sown with a winter cover crop. It is also conventional to plough the land either in the autumn or in early spring in preparation for the spring planting. By doing it early, the farmer can avoid having to wait for the soil to dry out before planting. However, early ploughing greatly increases the amount of winter and early spring erosion, decreasing the soil fertility and thus decreasing crop yields.

Ponds and Outlets
Farmers can install grassed outlets or ponds on their property to capture runoff before it reaches local waterways and to settle out the suspended solids and organic material. These function similarly to constructed wetlands, which are described in Chapter 9.

Changing Land Use
Sometimes the only solution to runoff in highly erodable areas is to take the land out of cultivation and plant it with a permanent cover of vegetation, converting it into grassland or woodland, for example.

TECHNIQUES FOR REDUCING FERTILIZER RUNOFF AND NITRATE LEACHING
The goal of any fertilization programme is to add enough nutrients to maximize plant productivity without wasting any fertilizer, either through surface runoff or leaching to ground-water. There are several effective best management practices to control nitrogen and phosphorus losses from cropland.

Nutrient Application Rates

It is important to match nutrient application rates to crop needs: heavy feeders such as maize and soybeans require more fertilizer than a nitrogen-fixing crop, for example. Using a slow-release chemical fertilizer will release nutrients over a period of days or weeks, so less goes to waste. Alternatively, composted manure can be used as a natural slow-release source of nutrients.

Timing of Nutrient Application

Fertilizer applications should correspond as closely as possible to plant needs by timing the application to coincide with the crop's active growing and flowering periods. This ensures the nutrients are taken up quickly and used completely. It is also important to take the weather into account, because fertilizers shouldn't be applied before a rainstorm, or applied to soil that is frozen.

Cover Crops and Crop Rotations

Carefully planned crop rotations can minimize nitrate leaching. Planting deep rooted crops following a shallow rooted crop will help to recover nitrate from the deeper soil zone. Using nitrogen-fixing crops in the annual rotation will increase the level of nitrogen in the soil so the next crop rotation will require much less fertilizer. This also reduces erosion risks, reduces leaching and improves soil structure.

Improved Water Management

Irrigation practices that result in large and uneven applications of water to soils greatly increase the risk of losses of mobile nitrate from the crop root zone. By making water application more uniform and efficient, by using above or below ground drip irrigation for example, nitrate losses are minimized.

TECHNIQUES FOR REDUCING PESTICIDE RUNOFF

Integrated pest management (IPM) is growing in popularity as a more cost-effective and environmentally sound method of pest control than traditional spraying regimes. The philosophy of IPM is to prevent or minimize the build-up of pests, so fewer pesticides are required to manage the pests if they do reach economically dangerous levels, rather than waiting until large outbreaks occur and then applying large volumes of pesticides. A variety of physical, cultural and biological techniques are involved. For example, IPM emphasizes using appropriate seeds: they should be weed- and disease-free, and pest-resistant crop varieties are preferred, even if the yield is lower than other varieties. Interspersing different crops and rotating crops helps to prevent the build-up of unwanted insects, and predatory or parasitic insects can be used to keep down the levels of pests. By following these practices, many farmers have been able to cut their pesticide use in half.

If pesticides are used, they should be applied according to the manufacturer's instructions. It is important to select the right weather conditions in order to minimize wind drift and water erosion, and to store and mix the chemicals properly to avoid spills or leakage.

Finally, agricultural chemicals can be eschewed entirely in favour of organic farming techniques that focus on building up a healthy soil, growing a diversity of crops to avoid the build-up of pests, and maintaining a population of beneficial insects that prey on pests.

TECHNIQUES FOR DEALING WITH ANIMAL WASTES

Modern animal rearing techniques such as beef feedlots and battery chicken rearing often produce highly concentrated wastes that must be handled appropriately. This means locating feeding and watering equipment a reasonable distance from streams and water-courses and away from flood plains to prevent surface runoff, and siting them on soil with a high clay content to ensure there is no danger of waste-water leaching into ground-water. If manure or feedlot runoff is applied to land, it should be done at appropriate rates so as not to risk leaching.

Chapter 6

Legislation and Economic Policies

Legislation

Governments can play an important role in preventing and controlling pollution, either through legislation or through economic policies. Legislation is the oldest, most widespread approach. It is sometimes referred to as the 'command and control' or 'regulatory' approach. The basic premise is that the state places restrictions on businesses and municipalities in order to reduce pollution. It monitors the businesses and municipalities to make sure they are complying with the regulations, or it establishes a system of self-reporting with periodic checks and audits, and it punishes any violations. Over time, the theory goes, regulations will create a 'climate of deterrence' that will discourage violations.

Legislation can take a number of forms. These include ambient standards, which establish permissible levels of pollutants in the environment; performance standards, which specify how much of a particular pollutant a business or municipality can release into the environment; and specification standards, which focus on the controlling of a particular process, rather than on the pollutants it produces, by requiring the implementation of 'best available technology'. Although legislation is often successful, it doesn't work in all situations. For it to be effective, it must be possible to readily identify the source of pollution, it should be relatively easy and inexpensive to monitor compliance, and there must be effective enforcement. For these reasons, legislation tends to be much more effective in regulating point source pollution than non-point source pollution. There are other drawbacks. From an economic perspective, legislation is not always equitable: the costs of complying with regulations can hit small businesses harder than large businesses. Nor is it cost-effective: legislation doesn't work unless there is effective enforcement, but enforcement doesn't come cheap, and court action is generally costly, cumbersome and time-consuming.

Finally, one of the fundamental problems of dealing with pollution in a free market economy is that businesses are not responsible for the costs of the pollution they create. In economic terms, the cost of pollution is an 'externality'. Traditionally, governments have compensated for this through legislation that restricts the volume or type of pollution. But businesses are constantly trying to minimize their costs. As long as the cost of not complying with pollution laws is less than the cost of complying, it makes more sense from an economic standpoint to pollute and pay the fines.

Economic Approaches

For all these reasons, there is a lot of interest in finding alternatives or supplements to the 'command and control' approach. For several decades, economists have suggested creating positive incentives to control pollution, through approaches such as product charges, taxes and tradable disposal permits (TDPs). By increasing the price of environmental resource inputs, governments can persuade industry to use them more efficiently. These 'market mechanisms' are effective, fast-acting and flexible.

PRODUCT CHARGES
If there is a strong link between the use of a particular product and an environmental impact, product charges can be an effective approach. Essentially, these are extra taxes put on products that pollute. In theory, the higher cost of these products will encourage businesses to look for non-polluting alternatives, and the taxes will be used to clean up the pollution the product causes. Product charges are particularly appropriate in dealing with non-point pollution such as the chemicals in agricultural runoff, which are a problem other policy instruments are not suited to deal with. The

Netherlands, Norway, Sweden, Finland, Austria and Denmark all have special taxes on fertilizers and/or pesticides.

TAXES

Taxation can take one of two forms: it can be either an incentive or a penalty. An incentive-based taxation policy offers firms tax incentives to reduce their pollution. This could be a tax exemption, for example, or a tax deferral. Canada, Finland, France and Switzerland offer tax reductions or accelerated depreciation for water pollution control equipment. The biggest advantage of incentive-based taxation, at least from the point of view of industry, is that it allows businesses to reduce pollution at a self-determined pace.

Penalty or 'Pigovian' taxation, named after the French economist A C Pigou, who first suggested it, is the imposition of taxes that compensate for the problem of externalities. A Pigovian is not a traditional tax in the sense that its goal is not to generate revenue; instead it is intended to alter behaviour. For example, governments can establish taxes based on the concentration of pollutants in industrial effluents. These 'water effluent charges' have been used successfully in Australia, France, Italy, the Netherlands, Germany, Belgium, Spain and Canada. One of the best examples of effluent charges is the policy of BOD charges in Germany's heavily industrialized Ruhr Valley. The tax discourages industries from releasing effluents with a high BOD, and income from the charge is used to finance treatment facilities. Since the implementation of the BOD charge, water quality in the Ruhr has improved significantly. The advantage of a tax is that it internalizes the cost of pollution, providing a positive incentive for firms to reduce their emissions. It creates an incentive for innovation and the development of new technology in pollution control, and it provides a source of revenue for government.

There are drawbacks to effluent charging schemes. Effluent charges still require monitoring, and therefore they are only suitable if a particular pollutant is easy to measure. They do not produce a predictable effect, and the tax may require a lot of fine tuning before the desired outcome is achieved. They condone pollution, sending a message to industry that it is OK to pollute. As critics point out, law carries with it the weight of positive moral sentiment; tax carries no moral weight. Probably the most important weakness is that effluent charges do not permit fine geographic control; while taxation may reduce overall rates of water pollution, it cannot protect small, vulnerable areas.

Finally, although environmental taxation offers a number of advantages, it can be a double-edged sword. In theory, generating revenue is not the primary objective of 'green taxation', but it does provide a source of government revenue. This creates a danger that government will become more interested in revenue than pollution reduction, and even become dependent on a certain level of pollution.

TDPs

TDPs are permits issued by the government entitling the owner to discharge one unit of pollution during a specific time period. This approach avoids the problems of setting charges in effluent charge systems; instead, the market determines prices for TDPs. The government establishes a target for total emissions and issues an appropriate number of permits. Dischargers can then buy and sell permits among themselves. Environmental groups can also buy up permits to take them off the market, thereby reducing the total amount of pollution.

Emissions trading is based on the premise that some discharges can reduce their emissions more easily and more cheaply than others. Those that can easily prevent pollution will reduce their emissions and sell off their excess TDPs. Others that would have to pay more to reduce their emissions or who are expanding their operations can buy these excess TDPs. Market forces will prevail. Any time the cost of pollution prevention is less than the income generated by selling TDPs, there is an economic incentive to reduce pollution. However, as with effluent charges, the biggest drawback to a TDP system is the lack of fine geographic control.

Public Pressure

Public pressure and education programmes are not substitutes for environmental regulations and enforcement. However, they are very valuable complementary approaches. They provide additional incentive and encouragement for businesses and municipalities to

---

Box 6.1 The Tar-Pamlico Trading Scheme

Over the past two decades, waterways in the Tar–Pamlico region of North Carolina have suffered from an overload of nutrients, caused largely by agricultural runoff. Local legislators decided something should be done. Although point sources accounted for only 17 per cent of the total nutrient load, they were the easiest target for regulation. The legislators therefore proposed to tighten restrictions on effluent from sewage treatment plants and industry.

The dischargers objected. Many had already spent considerable money on pollution control, and reducing their nutrient discharges even further would have little effect on water quality in the Tar–Pamlico basin. Instead, they offered an alternative. Since it would be more cost-effective for some point sources to reduce their discharges than others, and since it would be even more cost-effective for non-point sources to reduce runoff, they suggested a tradable permits scheme.

In 1989, the proposal was adopted. The local authorities set a strict limit on the total volume of nutrients that could be discharged in the basin, and issued a corresponding number of pollution permits to point source dischargers. However, the dischargers were free to buy and sell permits amongst themselves, or to pay into a fund to implement non-point pollution control in exchange for the right to continue to discharge.

The scheme proved successful. Between 1989 and 1993, nutrient loading was reduced by 28 per cent, even though industrial and residential expansion meant waste-water discharges actually increased by 18 per cent. Analyst David Riggs attributes this success to a number of factors, including the fact that the dischargers knew some form of pollution control was inevitable, the only question being what form it would take; the pollutant was common to all dischargers, making it simple to trade discharge permits; and there were differences in the cost of controlling the pollutant for different dischargers, both point and non-point, making trading economically desirable.

Source: Riggs (1993); Hall and Howett (1994)

---

comply with legislation, they are relatively inexpensive to implement and they don't require strong enforcement.

RIGHT-TO-KNOW LEGISLATION

'One of the most basic and powerful policies is that of a citizen's right to know what environmental risks are present in his or her community or workplace', according to James Post of the Boston University School of Management (Post, 1994, p 18). Right-to-know legislation includes laws that give the community access to public and private sector information on environmental issues, laws that ensure workers know about any toxic substances in the materials they handle, and laws that require the labelling of consumer products containing hazardous material.

One of the best examples of right-to-know legislation is the US Toxics Release Inventory (TRI). The TRI was enacted in 1986 as part of the Emergency Planning and Community Right-to-Know Act, and went on to become one of the most successful environmental laws in US history. The TRI is a simple pollution accounting system. It does not control how business manages waste, nor does it provide incentives. What it does is require major industrial plants to publicly disclose the levels of pollutants they discharge each year to air, water or land, or transfer to other sites for recycling or disposal.

Other countries have enacted similar legislation. In Canada, the National Pollutant Release Inventory requires facilities with more than ten employees to report releases of listed substances. The European Union has an audit scheme in which participating companies are issued environmental standards with audited release data, while the Netherlands has kept a registry of air and water releases since 1974. In the US experience, publishing pollution data motivates companies to reduce significantly their emissions for fear of community outcry. Several major companies, including Monsanto and Boeing, voluntarily reduced pollution by as much as 100 per cent after publication of TRI data. Often, they were not aware of the amount of pollution generated or of the costs of disposing of it, and the TRI data spurred them to change production methods.

CONSUMER PRESSURE

Consumers wield power at the checkout, and that power can influence the way businesses behave. Consumers can boycott products from a company with a poor environmental track record, or buy 'green' products that don't harm the environment. 'Eco-labelling' programmes give consumers the information they need to make environmentally sound choices. Such schemes can be initiated by governments, environmental groups or industry coalitions. They have proved quite successful: 'not tested on animals' labels improve the marketability of cosmetics and cleaners, for example.

Box 6.2 The British Example

Watershed management has been working in England and Wales for more than two decades. In the 1970s, the Central Advisory Water Committee concluded that the establishment of strong regional bodies based upon watersheds was 'absolutely necessary' in order effectively to solve the current and future water issues of England and Wales. In July 1973 the Water Act was passed, which reorganized the water industry along watersheds. It replaced more than 1600 separate water service entities with ten Regional Water Authorities, whose boundaries were defined by the watersheds of the country. Recently, the integrated approach has been taken one step further. In 1995, new legislation was passed which replaced the National Rivers Authority with a new government body that integrates air, land and water protection within a single unit, thus combining a watershed approach with a multimedia approach.

Source: Bulkley (1995)

Watershed Management

Currently, most water pollution control programmes are planned and implemented within political boundaries. This makes political, but not ecological, sense. The water flowing in a stream does not stop at the border of a state, nor does water pollution. Thus, in recent years, there has been a move towards watershed management, which tackles pollution in a comprehensive way within the natural boundaries of the watershed. There are, of course, barriers to the watershed approach. It requires communication, cooperation and conflict resolution across political boundaries, which is often no easy task. It also requires effort to build and maintain trust among the various levels of government, businesses and industries within the watershed. There are, however, successful examples.

Part III

Solutions

Chapter 7

Introduction to Ecological Technologies

There are a number of different natural treatment systems, some soil-based, some aquatic plant treatment systems. The next two chapters look at the details of the main types: slow-rate treatment, rapid infiltration, overland flow, constructed wetlands, floating aquatic plant systems and living machine systems. This chapter explores some of the common characteristics of natural systems, and the fundamental physical, chemical and biological mechanisms that underpin them.

Characteristics of Natural Systems

Conventional waste-water systems are energy- and chemical-intensive processes, designed primarily for large urban populations. They require trained operators and constant monitoring. They need energy to power massive aerators, to run mechanical mixing and scraping devices, and to fire the sludge incinerators. They need chlorine to disinfect the waste-water, or electricity to generate ozone or ultraviolet radiation. Finally, they need large volumes of concrete and steel to create the physical structure of the treatment plants. These high energy inputs make it possible for the treatment processes to occur within a relatively small land area at an accelerated pace, but they carry an environmental price tag. In contrast, 'natural systems' can be low cost, low energy solutions that work by recycling resources within a biological system. There are several different types of natural systems, but they all rely on some or all of the following basic components: water, soil, bacteria, higher plants and sunlight. They can achieve as good a level of treatment as conventional systems or better, without using lots of chemicals and without creating harmful byproducts.

Table 7.1 *Comparison of Natural Waste-water Treatment Technologies*

	Slow-rate treatment	*Rapid infiltration*	*Overland flow*	*Floating aquatic plant*	*Constructed wetlands*
Treatment goals	BOD TSS (total suspended solids) Nutrients	BOD TSS	BOD TSS Nutrients	BOD TSS Nutrients	BOD TSS Nutrients
Hydraulic loading (centimetres per day)	0.15–1.6	1.6–25	1–10	2–15	0.4–20
Area (hectares per thousand cubic metres per day)	6–67	0.4–6	1–10	0.7–5	0.5–20
Capital costs (US dollars per cubic metre per day)	800–2000	450–900	600–1000	500–1000	500–1000
Operating and mainte-nance costs (US dollars per cubic metre)	0.10–0.20	0.05–0.10	0.08–0.15	0.12–0.14	0.03–0.09

Source: Kadlec and Knight (1996)

On the down-side, natural systems usually take more time and more space to treat waste-water than do conventional systems. In most urban areas, where land is at a premium, this is a serious stumbling block. In addition, many natural systems slow down in the winter, which is a distinct disadvantage in northern temperate climates. Perhaps the biggest criticism of natural systems is their lack of a track record. Although there is a growing interest in natural sewage treatment, and more and more systems are being built, there is not yet a solid body of data on how they perform under a variety of conditions. Add to that a certain reluctance on the part of many civil engineers to trust a bunch of plants and soil to remove pollutants effectively, and you find substantial scepticism in the waste-water treatment industry about whether natural systems could reliably replace conventional technology. In fact, natural systems exploit many of the same processes used in conventional systems: sedimentation, filtration, gas transfer, adsorption, ion exchange, chemical precipitation, chemical oxidation and reduction, and biological conversion and degradation. In addition, they use photosynthesis, photooxidation, and plant uptake to remove pollutants. These processes occur at 'natural' rates, often simultaneously, rather than sequentially and at an artificially accelerated pace as they do in conventional systems.

Fundamental Mechanisms of Natural Systems

REMOVAL OF SUSPENDED SOLIDS

If suspended solids are not removed, they will cause turbidity in the receiving body of water, preventing sunlight from penetrating far into the water column and thus reducing the growth of plants and algae. They can also clog the gills of fish and suffocate bottom dwellers. The removal mechanisms used depend on the type of treatment system. In systems where waste-water flows above the soil surface (overland flow, wetlands, aquatic plant systems), suspended solids are removed by sedimentation. This can be enhanced by substantially slowing down the flow of the waste-water and reducing its depth. A portion of the suspended solids is also removed by filtration through the living vegetation and vegetative litter. In systems where waste-water flows below soil surface (slow-rate, rapid infiltration, vertical flow wetlands), suspended solids are filtered out as they pass through the soil or subsurface media. The biggest issue surrounding suspended solids in natural systems is the problem of particles clogging up pores in the media, thus preventing the waste-water from flowing through. For this reason, pretreatment settling ponds are often used to remove the bulk of suspended solids before the waste-water enters the treatment system.

MICROBIAL DECOMPOSITION OF ORGANIC MATERIAL

Microbial decomposition depends on the presence of bacteria, which are found on biofilms on the surfaces of plants and substrates. Some of these bacteria are aerobic, requiring oxygen to perform their work, while some are anaerobic and function without oxygen. Under anaerobic conditions, dissolved organic material is converted to methane, hydrogen sulphide, volatile fatty acids, carbon dioxide, etc – often a smelly process! Generally, designers of natural systems try to avoid anaerobic decomposition, except in situations where it is important to maximize nitrogen removal by denitrification (see Figure 7.1). For the most part, designers try to ensure the system remains aerobic so that organic material can be broken down without creating noxious odours. Under these conditions, organics are broken down into carbon dioxide, water, nitrates, phosphates, etc. Designers may use surface reaeration, photosynthetic oxygenation or mechanical aerators to provide oxygen for aerobic decomposition. However, it is not always easy to maintain aerobic conditions, so BOD is often the limiting design factor for water-based systems.

NITROGEN REMOVAL

Nitrogen commonly occurs in several forms, including nitrate, nitrite, ammonia and gaseous nitrogen. It can be readily converted from one form to another by aerobic and anaerobic bacteria through the process of nitrification/denitrification (see Figure 7.1).

It is important to remove both ammonia and nitrates during waste-water treatment to protect human and environmental health: ammonia is toxic to many fish and represents a significant oxygen demand on the receiving water, while nitrates cause eutrophication in receiving water and can cause 'blue baby' syndrome if they are present in drinking-water.

Nitrates are negatively charged particles that remain in solution. They are removed through several pathways. Some are taken up by plants, which incorporate the nutrient into their tissues. Some are converted into nitrogen gas by denitrifying bacteria in the absence

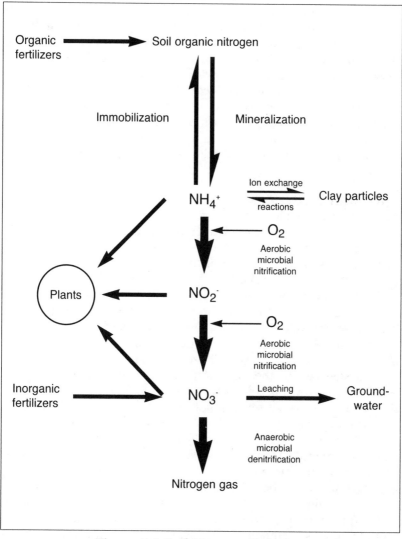

Figure 7.1 *Soil Nitrogen Pathways*

of oxygen. The gas then diffuses into the atmosphere. Finally, some can leach into underlying ground-water, although this may not be a desirable pathway in nitrate-sensitive areas. Many natural systems have liners to prevent leaching.

Ammonia is produced by the breakdown of the proteins found in sewage. Most ammonia is adsorbed temporarily through ion exchange reactions on soil particles and charged organic particles, and then nitrified by bacteria. Because these bacteria are aerobic, oxygen is a limiting step in nitrification. The nitrifiying bacteria also require warmth to work effectively: at temperatures under 5°C, they cease to function. Thus ammonia tends to be high in many natural systems during the winter. Some ammonia can also be removed by volatilization (although this is not desirable), and some by plant uptake, but these are relatively minor pathways.

Phosphorus Removal

Phosphorus occurs in a variety of forms, but the predominant one is orthophosphate (commonly referred to as simply 'phosphate'). Like nitrates, phosphates are an essential plant nutrient, and thus they can cause eutrophication if they are not removed before the waste-water is discharged into the body of receiving water. In natural systems, phosphorus removal occurs primarily through vegetation uptake, adsorption to soil particles and precipitation. Vegetation uptake can be significant in systems where the crops or vegetation are routinely harvested and removed. If the crops are not harvested, plant uptake will drop considerably.

In systems where the waste-water has the opportunity for extensive contact with soil, adsorption and precipitation reactions are the major pathways for phosphorus removal. Which specific reactions occur will depend on pH. At neutral to alkaline pH values, phosphorus precipitates chemically with calcium in the soil particles, while at acid pH values, it precipitates with iron or aluminium oxides. Phosphorus also adsorbs to clay minerals and certain organic fractions in the soil matrix. Once adsorbed, it is held tightly and is generally resistant to leaching. The total phophorus adsorption capacity of a given volume of soil is finite, but very large. Finer-textured soils tend to have the greatest potential for phosphorus sorption due to the higher clay content and also due to the increased hydraulic residence time. The sorption potential of a given soil layer will eventually be exhausted, but until that occurs, the removal of phosphorus will be almost complete.

DISINFECTION OF PATHOGENS

Many diseases are caused by waterborne pathogens: cholera, typhoid fever, bacterial dysentery, amoebic dysentery, poliomyelitis, infectious hepatitis and cryptosporidiosis, to name a few. In the interests of public health, it is clearly important to ensure these pathogens are removed during treatment. Some are easier to kill than others: most bacteria die off in a matter of days, for example, but parasitic cysts and eggs can persist for months. In water-based systems, pathogens are removed through natural die-off, predation, sedimentation and adsorption. Flatworm eggs, roundworm eggs and other parasitic cysts and eggs settle to the bottom. As a result, there is little risk of parasitic infections from pond effluents, but there may be some risk when sludges are removed for disposal.

Most land treatment systems are typically preceded by some form of preliminary treatment and/or a storage pond, so most pathogens are eliminated at this point. Bacteria and viruses are also removed in soil-based systems by a combination of filtration though the soil and vegetation, desiccation (in systems where waste-water is applied intermittently), adsorption to soil particles, ultraviolet radiation from the sun and predation by other microorganisms.

REMOVAL OF ORGANIC POLLUTANTS

This category includes a huge number of compounds that are a threat either to human health or to aquatic ecosystems, or both. It includes oils, pesticides, various industrial and household chemicals and waste products. Some organic pollutants are almost totally resistant to treatment and may persist in the environment for considerable periods of time; others are toxic or hazardous and require special management; while still others degrade quite readily. The principal methods for removing trace organics in natural treatment systems are volatilization to the atmosphere, adsorption to soil particles and biodegradation. In aquatic plant treatment systems, volatilization occurs at the water surface of wetlands, as it does in the pretreatment and storage ponds used in many soil-based systems. Volatilization also takes place in the water droplets from sprinklers used in land treatment, the liquid films in overland flow systems and the exposed surfaces of sludge. Because the quantities of pollutants involved are relatively small, volatilization should not pose any threat to workers in the vicinity. Adsorption occurs primarily on the organic matter in the treatment system. In many cases, bacteria and other microorganisms then degrade the adsorbed materials into simpler compounds, and ultimately into carbon dioxide and water.

METAL REMOVAL

Metals can be toxic both to humans and to aquatic organisms, and should be removed. In natural systems this can happen through several possible pathways. The largest percentage of the metals present in waste-water simply settles out with the suspended solids in the form of sludge. In aquatic plant treatment systems, a portion of the remaining metals adsorb onto organic matter. Finally, specific aquatic plants may take up metals. *Schoenoplectus spp.*, for example, accumulate copper, cobalt, nickel and manganese. Hyacinths can take up boron, copper, iron, manganese, lead, cadmium and chromium. Plant uptake also occurs in land treatment systems. In addition, metals are removed through adsorption, ion exchange, precipitation and complexation in or on the soil. Research has shown that metals in soil-based systems do not pose a threat to ground-water aquifers, even at the very high hydraulic loadings used in rapid infiltration systems.

Chapter 8

Soil-based Systems

'The rain to the river and the sewage to the soil.'

(Chadwick, quoted in NRC, 1996)

Rationale for Soil-based Treatment

Land disposal of sewage has a long history. After the advent of water carriage, human waste became a liquid problem, rather than a solid one. In the nineteenth century, sewage farms were developed to deal with this 'waste-water'. On these farms, located on the outskirts of cities, urban sewage was used both as an irrigator and as a manure to grow a variety of crops. Instead of discharging waste-water laden with nitrogen, phosphorus and organic material into waterways where it would cause pollution, it was used as a valuable resource to enrich and fertilize the soil. For example, at the turn of the century, Berlin had four farms totalling 19,000 acres. According to a contemporary US observer, they were run with 'military order' (Roechling, 1892). Sewage was pumped from the city to storage ponds at the highest point of each farm. The ponds could store large volumes of storm-water, as well as sewage, and release it slowly as the system was able to accommodate it. The ponds also served as settling basins to remove suspended solids. The waste-water flowed from the ponds through an extensive system of ditches that irrigated the farm. It percolated through the soil, adding organic material and nutrients to the fields, and was cleansed in the process. The enriched fields grew a variety of crops, including hay, wheat, barley, oats, turnips, potatoes, carrots and cabbages. The cleansed waste-water, now clear and sparkling, was collected in small underdrainage pipes and ultimately channelled to local watercourses. Although drinking the treated waste-water was officially prohibited, the workers labouring in the fields frequently drank from the collection ditches, apparently with no ill effect. Indeed, workers on the farms were reported to be as healthy as (or healthier than) the citizens of Berlin.

Sewage farms were used successfully by many cities for over half a century. However, as cities grew and began to encroach on the land, most were dismantled. Mismanagement of certain farms gave land disposal a bad name, and sanitary engineers began to preach the gospel of new, chemical methods. In the US it was not until the Water Quality Act of 1972 was passed that renewed interest was generated in land disposal. Twentieth century land disposal techniques have much in common with the old sewage farms. Land disposal is more effective than conventional secondary treatment, and the operation and maintenance costs are quite low, but it does require large areas of land. There are three main methods in use: slow-rate, rapid infiltration and overland flow. In all three methods, sewage is usually pretreated to remove suspended solids before it is applied to the land.

Slow-rate Treatment

Slow-rate treatment is the most widely used method for municipal and industrial waste-water: today there are over 800 operating slow-rate systems in the US alone. The technology is based on the methods of nineteenth century sewage farms, and is similar to conventional agricultural irrigation. The pretreated waste-water is sprinkled onto vegetated land on an intermittent schedule (see Figure 8.1), giving the soil time to re-aerate between applications. The waste-water is cleansed as it percolates vertically and horizontally through the soil. The vegetation also removes nutrients and filters out remaining solids, as well as keeping the soil permeable. Because of the large amounts of land required to distribute and treat the waste-water, these systems are generally the most costly of the soil-based treatment alternatives.

Slow-rate systems are suitable for a wide range of soil types and permeabilities. Optimal performance is achieved with a well drained loam soil. These systems should have a uniform depth of approximately 2 metres, to maintain aerobic conditions and prevent surface waterlogging. They should also have a minimum depth of 2 metres to ground-water to avoid problems with leaching. A wide variety of crops can be grown in slow-rate systems, depending on which nutrients need to be removed (see Table 8.1).

Table 8.1 *Nutrient Uptake Rates for Selected Plants (kilograms per hectare per year)*

Plant	Nitrogen	Phosphorus	Potassium
Forage crops			
Alfalfa	225–675	22–34	174–224
Brome grass	130–224	40–56	247
Coastal bermuda grass	400–675	35–45	225
Kentucky bluegrass	200–270	45	200
Quack grass	235–280	30–45	275
Reed canary grass	335–450	40–45	315
Ryegrass	200–280	60–85	270–325
Sweet clover	175–300	20–40	100–300
Tall fescue	150–325	30	300
Orchard grass	250–350	20–50	225–315
Timothy	140	24	200
Vetch	390	46	270
Field crops			
Barley	125–160	15–25	20–120
Maize	175–250	20–40	110–200
Cotton	75–180	15–28	40–100
Grain sorghum	135–250	15–40	70–170
Oats	115	17	120
Potatoes	230	20	245–325
Rice	110	26	125
Soybeans	250–325	10–28	30–120
Sugarbeets	255	26	450
Wheat	160–175	15–30	20–160

Source: Reed *et al.* (1995)

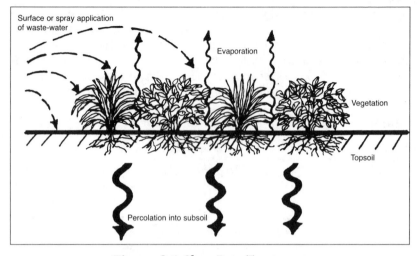

Figure 8.1 *Slow-Rate Treatment*

There are two basic approaches to slow-rate treatment. In a Type 1 system, the goal is to treat waste-water as efficiently as possible, so the maximum possible amount of waste-water is applied to the smallest possible land area. The limiting factor in this scenario is usually the hydraulic capacity of the soil profile or the nitrogen content of the waste-water. The Type 2 approach is to emphasize reusing the waste-water, and the goal is to grow a good yield of crops. Waste-water is used to irrigate the maximum possible amount of land, by adding just enough water to satisfy the total irrigation requirement of the crop being grown. In areas where irrigation water is in short supply but land is readily available, Type 2 systems make good sense. The main disadvantage of slow-rate systems is the amount of land required. Because they have the lowest loading rate of land treatment methods, they require the greatest area of land. Most slow-rate systems also require some storage for periods during cold or wet weather, and during crop planting and harvesting. In addition they require a certain amount of maintenance: the crops must be planted, cultivated and harvested on a seasonal basis; the soil must be managed to keep it well drained and functioning at optimal pH; and some potassium may need to be added for good crop growth. Slow-rate systems are functionally similar to the septic tank and leach field systems used by many households in rural areas. The septic tank provides pre-treatment settling, while the leachfield is a series of perforated pipes in underground trenches that discharge the waste-water to the surrounding soil.

Rapid Infiltration Systems

In rapid infiltration systems, the pretreated waste-water is applied intermittently to shallow infiltration basins or ponds, where it percolates into the surrounding soil (see Figure 8.2). Suspended solids are removed by filtration through the soil matrix, and nitrogen is removed through nitrification/denitrification. Because of the small land area required and the relative ease of periodically applying waste-water to the basins, this technology is the least expensive method of land disposal. Depending on the design objectives, the treated waste-water can be allowed to seep into the underlying ground-water or it can be recovered through wells or underdrains. There are approximately 300 municipal rapid infiltration systems currently operating in the US. Rapid infiltration systems require sand, sandy loams, loamy sands or gravels, and a minimum of 5 metres of well drained soil. The minimum depth to ground-water should be 5 metres. They can handle hydraulic loading rates of 6–125 metres per year, significantly higher than the loading rates for slow-rate systems. The lower the hydraulic loading rate, the better the treatment level achieved, especially for nitrogen and phosphorus removal. Ammonia removal can be readily accomplished through nitrification. These systems can operate successfully on a year-round basis, as long as ice formation in or on the upper soil profile is avoided. The only maintenance required is to scrape the surface of the basin periodically.

Overland Flow Systems

Overland flow systems are suited to areas where the soil is relatively impermeable. The pretreated waste-water is applied intermittently to the top of carefully graded, vegetated slopes, often using high pressure sprinklers (see Figure 8.3). Because it can't percolate into the soil, the waste-water flows over the surface of the slope and

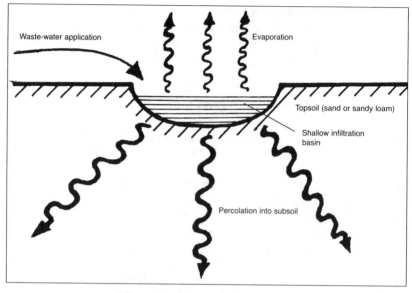

Figure 8.2 *Rapid Infiltration*

through the dense vegetation. Suspended solids are filtered out by the vegetation, or they settle out and degrade at the soil surface. Nutrients are taken up by the plants, and pathogens die off in the inhospitable environment. The cleansed waste-water is collected in ditches at the bottom. During cold weather and periods of heavy rainfall the waste-water must be stored in lagoons so the system is not overloaded. In the US, these systems were used almost exclusively in food processing industries until the mid 1970s. Since then, they have been used successfully for municipal waste-water as well, and today there are approximately 50 municipal overland flow systems nation-wide. Such systems can be designed to achieve secondary, advanced secondary or tertiary nutrient removal, depending on the treatment requirements. Even stricter standards can be met if the waste-water is pretreated to a higher level, or if it is applied at lower loading rates. Annual loading rates vary between 3 and 20 metres per year.

Unlike other land treatment systems, overland flow requires heavy clays or clay loams, with a minimum of 15–20 centimetres of topsoil, and there should be a minimum of 1.5 metres of soil

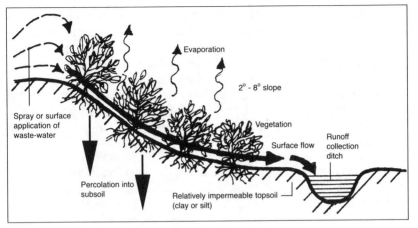

Figure 8.3 *Overland Flow*

Box 8.1 Werribee Farm

Werribee Farm is a 27,000 acre modern sewage farm in Melbourne, Australia. It was established in 1897 and continues to operate successfully today. It treats 440,000 cubic metres of sewage per day and produces forage crops for cattle and sheep.

Three methods of purification are used: slow-rate treatment, overland flow and lagooning. Slow-rate treatment is used during late spring, summer and autumn when evaporation rates are high and the fields require irrigation. Overland flow is employed during the winter when evaporation rates are low and there is no need for irrigation. Lagoons, both aerobic and anaerobic, are used year-round to buffer the system from peak inflows of waste-water: both daily peak flows and high flows in wet weather.

The farm is divided into a number of pasture bays. Each bay is irrigated for 1 or 2 days, followed by 5–8 days of drying, and 10–14 days of livestock grazing. The farm supports 22,000 beef cattle and 30,000 sheep.

The system is highly effective at removing nutrients, suspended solids, organic material and heavy metals. The cost is US$1.53 per capita per year, and annual sales of meat bring in a good income.

Unfortunately, urban development is encroaching on the system. As residential development increases near the farm, odour from the overland flow treatment site is becoming more of a problem. For this reason, the system is being converted from the application of raw sewage to the application of pretreated sewage.

overlying the ground-water. The grass used on overland flow slopes performs a number of key functions: it provides a support medium for microorganisms, it minimizes erosion, and it takes up nitrogen and phosphorus. A mixture of different grass types is usually used. Overland flow systems require minimal management – cutting the grass two or three times a year. The biggest difficulty in overland flow systems is ensuring the slope is steep enough to prevent the waste-water from forming ponds but isn't so steep that erosion becomes a problem.

Table 8.2 *Performance Data for Werribee Farm*

Pollutant	Percentage removal
BOD	99
Suspended solids	98
Nitrogen	95
Phosphorus	95
Zinc	95
Copper	95
Lead	95
Chromium	90
Cadmium	85
Mercury	85
Nickle	75

Source: Loehr *et al.* (1979); Feigin *et al.* (1991)

Performance

Generally speaking, soil-based systems perform quite well (see Table 8.3). Slow-rate systems offer the best removal rates for the common pollutants. Rapid infiltration and overland flow systems are less effective at removing metals, and rapid infiltration systems perform relatively poorly at nitrogen removal. All systems are very good at removing organic chemicals (see Table 8.4).

The biggest problem associated with the use of land treatment systems is hydraulic overloading. Too high a volume of waste-water creates waterlogged soil and harms the vegetation. Ultimately this

Table 8.3 *Removal Efficiencies (per cent) of Major Constituents for Municipal Land Application Systems*

Constituent	Slow-rate	Rapid infiltration	Overland flow
BOD	98	85–99	92
COD	95	50	80
Suspended solids	98	98	92
Total nitrogen	85	0–50	70–90
Total phosphorus	80–99	60–95	40–80
Metals	95	50–95	50
Microorganisms	95	98	98

Source: Honachefsky (1991)

means the system cannot work effectively, leading to the contamination of ground-water and surface-waters. Thus it is critical to monitor the loading rates on an ongoing basis so as not to overload the system.

A second problem concerns the potential for soil-based systems to transmit pathogens off-site. This could occur in a number of ways: via contaminated vegetation, off-site runoff, leaching to ground-water or aerosols. To eliminate the risk of contaminated vegetation, agricultural land treatment sites are not used to grow crops that might be eaten raw. Sites are carefully designed to minimize off-site runoff and leaching to ground-water. In slow-rate and overland flow systems that rely on sprinklers to apply the waste-water, aerosol droplets can be formed and carried off in the wind, creating a potential health risk to neighbouring properties. Many jurisdictions now require substantial buffer zones around rapid infiltration and overland flow systems to avoid contaminating adjoining land.

Finally, there is the issue of metals. In soil-based systems, metals are removed by a number of pathways, one of which is plant uptake. In theory, then, consuming these metal-contaminated plants could pose a potential health risk. In practice, this is highly unlikely: most metals are toxic to plants long before the concentration reaches levels that are toxic to humans. Even cadmium, which can accumulate to dangerous levels without killing the plant, does

Table 8.4 *Removal of Organic Chemicals (per cent) in Land Treatment Systems*

Chemical	Slow-rate sandy soil	Slow-rate silty soil	Overland flow	Rapid infiltration
Chloroform	98.57	99.23	96.50	99.99
Toluene	>99.99	>99.99	99.00	99.99
Benzene	>99.99	>99.99	98.09	>99.99
Chlorobenzene	99.97	99.98	98.99	>99.99
Bromoform	99.93	99.96	97.43	>99.99
Dibromochlor- methane	99.72	99.72	98.78	>99.99
M-nitrotoluene	>99.99	>99.99	94.03	NA
PCB 1242	>99.99	>99.99	96.46	>99.99
Napthalene	99.98	99.98	98.49	96.15
Phenanthrene	>99.99	>99.99	99.19	NA
Pentachlorophenol	>99.99	>99.99	98.06	NA
2,4-dinitrophenol	NA	NA	93.44	NA
Nitrobenzene	>99.99	>99.99	88.73	NA
M-dichlorobenzene	>99.99	>99.99	NA	82.27
Pentane	>99.99	>99.99	NA	NA
Hexane	99.96	99.96	NA	NA
Diethylphthalate	NA	NA	NA	90.75

Note: The removals reported for slow-rate systems represent concentrations in the applied waste-water ranging from 2 to 111 micrograms per litre; the applied concentrations in the overland flow system ranged from 25 to 315 micrograms per litre; and in the rapid infiltration system, they ranged from 2 to 89 micrograms per litre.
Source: Reed *et al.* (1995)

not appear to pose a risk. Research at the Werribee Farm in Melbourne, Australia, found that after 76 years of application of raw sewage, cadmium concentrations in the grass were only slightly higher than concentrations in grass from control sites.

Land Application of Sludge

Sludge is the semi-solid material settled out from sewage by conventional sewage treatment. (More recently the industry has begun to refer to it as 'biosolids' in a bid to make the product sound more palatable.) Sludge is 3–10 per cent organic and inorganic solids; the rest is water. The composition of the solids varies depending on the type of waste-water and the treatment process, but the main components are partially decomposed organic matter and significant amounts of plant nutrients. In addition, there may be traces of heavy metals and organic chemicals from industrial effluent, as well as pathogens.

Sludge disposal is one of the big headaches of conventional sewage treatment. What do you do with thousands of tonnes of semi-solid material each day, particularly if it is contaminated with heavy metals and industrial chemicals? This problem is only going to get worse in the coming years as the demand for cleaner water forces countries to adopt higher treatment standards; the higher the level of waste-water treatment provided, the more sludge is produced. For example, in 1994, the European Union produced approximately 6.5 million tonnes of dry sludge solids. As new European legislation comes into effect, major improvements to sewage treatment will be required, resulting in the generation of much more sludge. At the same time, more restrictions are being placed on sludge disposal.

There are four basic methods for getting rid of sludge: incineration, landfill, sea disposal and application to land (see Table 8.5). The first three merely transfer the problem to another media – dumping it in the water, in the air, or on the ground without attempting to reclaim any of the valuable nutrients or organic matter. Legislators are beginning to recognize the inefficiency of these approaches. In Europe curbs are now being imposed on landfill, incinerators must now meet stricter emission regulations and disposal at sea has been banned. Applying sludge to land is one of the more attractive options remaining.

Applying sludge to land has a number of benefits. Sludge improves the quality of the soil by boosting the organic matter content and hence improving the soil's capacity to hold water. Sludge also improves plant growth: as it decomposes, sludge releases nitrogen, phosphorus, sulphur, calcium, magnesium and

Table 8.5 *Sludge Disposal in Europe*

Country	Agriculture (per cent)	Landfill (per cent)	Incineration (per cent)	Sea (per cent)	Total volume (thousands of tonnes per year)
Belgium	14	76	10	0	29
Germany (West)	32	59	9	0	2180
Denmark	43	30	27	0	131
France	28	52	20	0	850
Greece	0	100	0	0	15
Ireland	30	17	0	52	23
Italy	34	55	11	0	800
Luxembourg	80	20	0	0	15
The Netherlands	64	28	3	5	199
Spain	62	10	0	28	280
England and Wales	53	16	7	24	958
Sweden	60	40	–	–	180
Switzerland	45	32	23	–	250
Austria	29	34	37	–	198

Source: Journal of the Institute of Water and Environmental Management, 1992, p 552.

other important plant nutrients. Studies have shown that crops grown on land that is enriched with sewage sludge produce high yields, and the quality of those yields is high. If sludge is applied to forested areas, it increases the growth of trees. Sludge can also be used to reclaim strip-mine spoils, mine tailings and gravel spills.

Sludge can be applied to land without any form of treatment, but generally it is processed in some way to reduce the volume and avoid problems with odours and pathogens. It can be applied in dried, composted or liquid forms. In Europe sludge is typically applied as a digested liquid, either sprayed from a truck or applied in the furrows between ridges of crops. Another approach is to add dewatered and composted sludge to the land in thin layers using a truck spreader and ploughing the sludge under the soil after it has

Table 8.6 *Typical Values of Nitrogen, Phosphorous and Potassium as Percentage of Total Solids*

Element	Digested sludge	Milorganite	Typical lawn fertilizer
Nitrogen	3.0	6.0	9
Phosphorus	2.5	2.0	3
Potassium	0.5	0	3

Adapted from Sincero and Sincero (1996)

dried. Several US cities bag and sell processed municipal sludge as compost: Milwaukee has treated and dried its sludge and sold it as 'Milorganite' fertilizer for many years, and Philadelphia markets its sludge as 'Philagrow' (see Table 8.6). All municipal sludge in Washington, DC, has been applied to land (including the White House lawn) since 1974.

There are some concerns about applying sludge to land, particularly land used to grow food crops. The biggest worries are contaminating the soil, the crops or the underlying ground-water with the heavy metals, synthetic organic compounds, nitrates or pathogens that are often present in sludge. Some of these fears have proved unfounded. Most organic compounds are rapidly adsorbed, volatilized or decomposed, so they do not present a risk to the food chain. Soil adsorption and climatic conditions are quite effective at killing pathogens (see Table 8.7).

Table 8.7 *Survival Time of Pathogens in Soil and on Plant Surfaces*

Pathogen	Soil		Plant	
	Absolute max.	Common max.	Absolute max.	Common max.
Bacteria	1 year	2 months	6 months	1 month
Viruses	6 months	3 months	2 months	1 month
Protozoan cysts	10 days	2 days	5 days	2 days
Helminth eggs	7 years	2 years	5 months	1 month

Source: Sincero and Sincero (1996)

Table 8.8 *Typical Mean Concentrations of Heavy Metals and Toxic Elements in Sludges (Milligrams per Litre)*

Silver	230	Mercury	10
Arsenic	10	Manganese	2000
Boron	420	Nickel	400
Barium	1500	Lead	2000
Cadmium	90	Strontium	450
Cobalt	360	Selenium	30
Chromium	1700	Vanadium	500
Copper	1300	Zinc	4000

Source: Sincero and Sincero (1996)

Heavy metals are more controversial (see Table 8.8). Studies have shown that soils with neutral to alkaline pH sequester heavy metals, making them unavailable to plants, and that at the volumes applied to agricultural land, sludge does not significantly increase the heavy metal content of crops or impair their quality. However, problems can occasionally arise if large volumes of sludge are applied to land, overwhelming the soil's adsorption capacity, or if the soil is excessively acidic, causing heavy metals to be released.

Nitrates too can leach into ground-water if more sludge is applied to land than the crops can handle. For these reasons, most countries have regulations about how much sludge can be applied to land, and what kind of land is suitable for sludge disposal. In Europe, disposal to land is being carefully restricted to prevent metals, nitrates and phosphorus from leaching into ground-water or running off into surface-waters. In the US, sludge cannot be applied to any site with a soil pH less than 6.5, sand or sandy loam soils, a high water table or a slope of more than 12 per cent.

An alternative approach, recommended in a recent European Union study, is to establish 'common and demanding' standards for industrial effluents discharged to sewers, sufficiently tight so that all sludges would be suitable for disposal to agricultural land. In essence, this means strict source control (see Chapter 5) (ENDS Report, 1995). Industries would no longer be permitted to discharge metals and chemicals into municipal sewers; instead, they would be forced to recycle them, reuse them or dispose of them safely.

Chapter 9

Aquatic Plant Treatment Systems

The philosophy behind aquatic plant treatment systems arises from observations that many natural aquatic systems such as ponds and wetlands have an inherent ability to cleanse waste-water. This knowledge has been translated into the development of a variety of constructed aquatic plant treatment systems designed specifically to remove pollutants from waste-water. These systems fall into three basic categories: constructed wetlands, floating aquatic plant systems and living machine systems.

Constructed Wetlands

Wetlands are areas that are wet or waterlogged for at least part of the year, such as swamps, marshes, bogs and fens. Generally, wetlands have not been highly valued. Across North America and Europe, thousands of acres have been drained and turned into agricultural land or commercial and residential developments. Only recently have we begun to recognize the value of wetlands, their remarkable ability to cleanse water and their vital role in natural ecosystems.

Research into the cleansing ability of wetlands began in the 1950s when German scientists Käthe Seidel (1978) and Reinhold Kickuth (1970) first investigated the possibility of using wetlands to remove nutrients and suspended solids from polluted water. Seidel proved that bulrushes (*Schoenoplectus lacustris*) could remove large quantities of organic and inorganic substances from contaminated water. In later studies, she demonstrated that bulrushes can also reduce the levels of bacteria in waste-water by secreting natural antibiotic substances from their roots, and they can sequester heavy metals and eliminate hydrocarbons. Interest in this work spread from Germany across Europe, to North America, Australia and around the world. Today hundreds of natural and constructed wetlands are used to treat waste-water and storm-water as far north as the Yukon and the Northwest Territories in Canada and as far south as Australia and New Zealand. The systems range in size from very small systems designed to treat the waste-water of a single household to reasonably large systems such as one constructed wetland in Mexico that treats the waste-water of more than 100,000 people.

DESIGN

Because natural wetlands are often fragile ecosystems that could be stressed by being exposed to too many pollutants, it is better to design and build wetlands specifically for the purpose of treating waste-water. These systems are known as constructed wetlands or reed beds. They have three key components: plants, microbes and substrate. Water-tolerant plants are rooted in a soil or gravel substrate and the system is saturated with water. The substrate supports the plants, while the roots of the plant provide a home for a variety of microbes.

Almost any species of aquatic plant is suitable for a wetland system; the most popular are common reeds (*Phragmites australis*), cattails (*Typha* spp.), and grasses (*Scirpus* spp.). Certain plants, such as common reeds and cattails, have hollow stems that can transport air to the roots, supplying the microbes with additional oxygen. Some take up specific metals or chemicals, others produce an exudate that kills pathogens.

It takes approximately 1–2 square metres of wetland to treat the waste-water of one person. This is accomplished through a combination of physical, chemical and biological processes:

- suspended solids settle to the bottom in still water or are filtered by the wetland substrates and the plants
- organic material is broken down by microbes that live on the roots of the plants
- nitrates can be transformed by denitrifying bacteria to nitrogen gas, or they can be taken up by the plants

Table 9.1 *List of Commonly Used Plants and Their Properties*

Phragmites australis (common reeds) and *Typha* spp. (cattails):
- flocculate colloids, eliminate pathogens

Schoenoplectus spp. (bulrushes):
- take up copper, cobalt, nickel, manganese, chlorinated hydrocarbons
- eliminate pathogens
- exude antibiotics

Scirpus spp. (grasses):
- break down phenols
- eliminate pathogens

Juncus spp. (rushes):
- treat chlorinated hydrocarbons, cyanide compounds, phenols
- remove pathogens

Iris pseudocorus (yellow flag):
- remove pathogens

Adapted from Mollison, 1988

- ammonia is transformed by bacteria to nitrates
- phosphorus precipitates with calcium, iron and aluminium compounds; it is removed both by sedimentation and adsorption to the soil and by plant uptake
- metals and toxic chemicals are removed by oxidation, precipitation and plant uptake
- pathogens die off in the inhospitable environment and are ingested by other organisms, or are killed off by antibacterial compounds (although wildlife in the wetland may introduce more)

The design and layout of the system will depend on the local topography, the nature of the incoming waste-water and the specific treatment objectives. How much land is required will depend on input loading of pollutants, wetland design and treatment objectives, but, generally speaking, the higher the loading or the higher the degree of treatment desired, the larger the area of land that will be required.

There are two types of constructed wetland systems: surface flow wetlands and subsurface flow wetlands. In addition, subsurface flow systems can be broken down into horizontal flow wetlands and vertical flow wetlands.

Surface Flow Wetlands

Surface flow wetlands are usually shallow impoundments, lined with impermeable material, that are filled with a soil or gravel substrate and planted with emergent vegetation (see Figure 9.1). They are designed to be flooded, so the water level lies above the surface of the substrate, and waste-water therefore flows above the substrate and through the dense stands of plants. In this sense they mimic the flow of water in natural wetlands. Surface flow wetlands are relatively cheap to build (US$10,000–100,000 per hectare, depending on the size of the system); the major cost is earthwork.

Subsurface Flow Wetlands

Subsurface flow wetlands are similar to surface flow wetlands, but are designed so the waste-water flows through the substrate rather than above it. The water level is therefore maintained below the surface of the substrate. Subsurface flow systems are better suited to cooler climates than surface flow wetlands because much of the treatment occurs below the ground surface, where conditions are generally warmer than above ground during the winter. This, combined with the warmth of the incoming waste-water, prevents the beds from freezing in subzero conditions. They are also less likely to have odour or mosquito problems than surface flow wetlands, and they can handle higher loadings of waste-water. However, they have a tendency to plug up if the organic loading is too high. Because of this, it is common for subsurface flow systems to be preceded by a settlement stage to remove suspended solids. In addition, multiple inlets are often used to disperse the suspended solids as evenly as possible and avoid the problems of clogging. Subsurface flow wetlands are more expensive to build (four to eight times the cost of a surface flow system), in large part because of the cost of gravel fill.

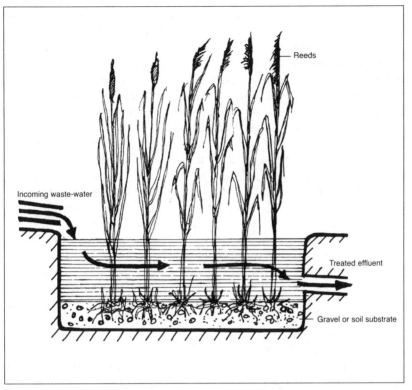

Figure 9.1 *Surface Flow Wetland*

Subsurface flow systems can be designed for horizontal or vertical flow (see Figure 9.2). The horizontal flow system (sometimes referred to as the Kikuth or Root Zone Method) was pioneered by Dr R Kikuth in the mid 1960s. It comprises a rectangular bed of light clay or heavy soil planted with *Phragmites australis*. Calcium and iron or aluminium supplements are often added to improve the soil structure and increase the capacity of the soil to precipitate phosphates. It is designed so the waste-water flows horizontally through the rhizosphere of the reeds.

Initially these systems were very popular, and hundreds were installed across Europe and the UK. Unfortunately, there were certain problems with the design. To function properly, the horizontal systems depend on a high degree of porosity in the soil to allow the waste-water to flow properly. Kikuth believed that, over time, the porosity of the soil would increase as the roots of the reeds extended through the soil and then died, creating pores through which waste-water could flow. Several decades of experience have proved this is not the case, and many problems have been encountered with waste-water flowing across the soil surface because the soil was not sufficiently permeable. To get around this problem, gravel is now widely used as the substrate in horizontal flow systems, rather than soil. Gravel is particularly suitable when hydraulic loadings are high and space is at a premium. Although effective at reducing BOD and suspended solids, horizontal flow systems struggle with nitrification of ammonia due to their relatively anoxic conditions. Pathogen removal is excellent.

There has been a gradual move in favour of vertical flow beds in recent years. In these systems, waste-water is applied to the surface of the bed in intermittent doses and percolates vertically through the substrate, which is usually gravel. Intermittent dosing encourages oxygenation of the substrate and this oxygenated environment allows for higher levels of BOD reduction and greater nitrification of ammonia. The plants form a mat on the surface of the bed, trapping the suspended solids which then degrade aerobically. The bacteria in the substrate provide further treatment as the effluent trickles through. Using gravel as a substrate avoids the conductivity problems encountered with the soil-based horizontal systems, while the alternate wet and dry periods enhance the fixation of phosphorus in the substrate.

Although vertical flow beds are now widely accepted as the better system, there are some situations in which horizontal flow systems may be the most suitable option. For example, horizontal systems may be installed if the levels of BOD and total suspended solids (TSS) must be reduced to secondary treatment standards, but ammonia nitrification is not required. Horizontal flow systems are also useful in removing nitrate by biological denitrification under anoxic or anaerobic conditions.

It can also be advantageous to combine horizontal and vertical flow systems, and this is often done to provide a complete secondary treatment. Most thorough treatment occurs if effluent passes first through a vertical flow system and then through a horizontal flow system. Aerobic bacteria in the vertical flow system

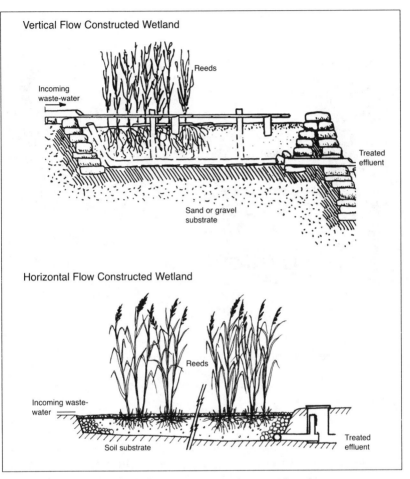

Figure 9.2 *Subsurface Flow Wetlands*

nitrify ammonia to nitrate, and bacteria adapted to the anoxic conditions in the horizontal flow system denitrify nitrates to nitrites and nitrogen gas. The retention time for effluent in the vertical flow system is short, so for effective pathogen removal, it is best to have a much longer retention time in the horizontal flow system.

In North America, roughly two-thirds of constructed wetlands are surface flow systems, while in Europe, the preference is for subsurface flow systems.

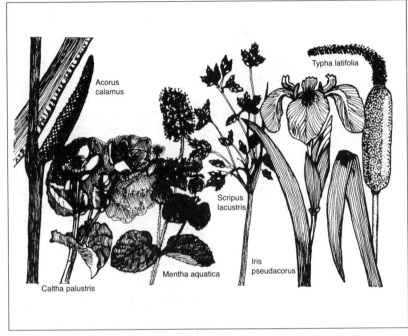

Figure 9.3 *Common Plants in Constructed Wetlands*

PERFORMANCE

Wetlands offer several advantages over conventional systems. First, they are cheap to build and cheap to run, so long as land is readily available. Secondly, they are effective at treating waste-water – in fact, more effective at removing certain pollutants than conventional treatment systems. They are also more flexible and less susceptible to variations in loading rates than conventional treatment systems, coping particularly well with shock loadings. Finally, they create wildlife habitat and green space. On the down side, wetlands require lots of land. This may not be a problem in rural areas, but it can be a big stumbling block in cities where land is at a premium (although wetland advocates point out that if cities can pipe drinking-water from sources hundreds of kilometres away, there is no reason why they can't pipe waste-water similar distances to rural areas where land is more readily available).

Table 9.2 *Performance Data for an Average Constructed Wetland*

Constituent	In (milligrams per litre)	Out (milligrams per litre)	Removal efficiency (per cent)
BOD	38.8	10.5	73
Suspended solids	49.1	15.3	69
Ammonia	7.5	4.2	44
Total nitrogen	14	5	64
Total phosphorus	4.2	1.9	55

Source: Pries (1994)

Reports on how effectively constructed wetlands remove pollutants vary considerably, from virtually nil to greater than 90 per cent but generally they are good (see Table 9.2). Many of the poor results can be attributed to systems that are overloaded, poorly managed, poorly designed, optimized for the removal of different pollutants or not yet fully established. Several researchers suggest that the variability in performance should not be interpreted to mean that wetlands are unreliable or unpredictable, but indicates a need for widely accepted design criteria.

Wetlands may not always operate at peak efficiency. Because they depend on plant and microbial action, peak removal efficiencies are not reached until the vegetation is well established, which can take a few seasons. This also means that in temperate climates they do not work as efficiently in winter as they do in summer, particularly in terms of nitrogen removal. The cold temperatures slow down reactions, and the plants die off or become dormant. However, the microorganisms remain active on the plant roots throughout the winter, and the system as a whole continues to function at reduced efficiency.

Another disadvantage is that wetlands are a relatively new technology. As noted above, standard criteria for design, construction and operation need to be developed. The most common difficulty encountered in soil-based wetland systems is keeping the soil partially aerated, particularly in the case of horizontal flow beds. When constructed wetlands are overloaded by oxygen-demanding constituents or too great a depth of water, there is not enough oxygen for the system to function effectively. The results are unhealthy plants and decreased removal of BOD and ammonia.

Finally, there is an unresolved question of the life expectancy of constructed wetlands: how long they can continue to remove pollutants at an optimal rate. In theory, this is a particularly critical issue when it comes to phosphorus removal, because the concentration of phosphorus will gradually build up in the soil until a saturation point is reached. In practice, the oldest constructed wetlands have operated for decades without reaching phosphate saturation.

MAINTENANCE AND UPKEEP

There are a number of tasks involved in the management of constructed wetland systems. First of all, if several beds are being used in parallel, the stream of incoming waste-water should be shifted periodically from bed to bed. The systems may need to be flushed out occasionally and the whole system should be monitored regularly to ensure it isn't being overloaded. Like any waste-water treatment system, the effluent should be tested on an ongoing basis to measure the performance of the system and ensure the discharge criteria are being met. Finally, the vegetation requires occasional attention: planting, weeding and seasonal harvesting.

APPLICATIONS

Constructed wetlands are used to treat a wide variety of waste-waters, including municipal waste-water, industrial waste-water, agricultural runoff, urban storm-water, landfill leachate, pulp and paper effluent and acid mine drainage. They can be designed for specific climatic conditions, the characteristics of the incoming waste-water, the quality of effluent required and the nature of the land available. A few examples are listed below.

Municipal Waste-water

Constructed wetlands are most widely used to treat municipal waste-water. They have been used successfully to treat both primary and secondary effluent from activated sludge and lagoon systems, as well as septic tank effluent. In North America, constructed wetlands are most commonly used to provide tertiary treatment for municipal waste-water from larger urban centres. In contrast, European systems are generally used in small towns and villages to provide secondary level treatment. Some jurisdictions have a deliberate policy of using constructed wetlands to treat municipal waste-water. In the English Midlands and in Wales, the local water company installs constructed wetlands in communities of less than 2000 wherever tertiary treatment is required. As a result, almost 100 small community sewage treatment plants now use constructed wetlands to polish secondary effluent and treat storm-water overflows.

Urban Storm-water
Surface flow wetlands are highly effective and widely used for treating urban storm-water. They improve the quality of the water by breaking down many of the pesticides, organic compounds, oils and greases found in storm-water. They also modify flow rates by storing the water temporarily, thus attenuating flow and allowing suspended solids a chance to settle out. Often the wetlands are arranged as a series of detention ponds or infiltration basins.

Agricultural Runoff
Although there is less published information about using constructed wetlands to treat agricultural storm-water or feedlot runoff, there are several successful examples. One simple approach is to build a buffer of wetlands between agricultural land and streams, rivers or ponds. In Ontario, several projects are under way that use constructed wetlands to filter runoff from farm feedlots and discharge from milkhouse wash-water before they reach local watercourses.

Industrial Waste-water
There are many potential industrial applications for wetlands. Constructed wetlands can be used to remove metals, adjust pH, reduce BOD and filter suspended particles. For example, they are used to treat waste-water from the dairy industry and meat processing and rendering plants, storm-water runoff from coal and ash piles, pulp and paper effluent and acidic drainage water from mines (acid mine drainage).

DEBATE: ROLE OF PLANTS IN CONSTRUCTED WETLANDS

There is a certain amount of controversy about the significance of the role played by plants in waste-water treatment. While some researchers believe plants are an essential part of constructed wetlands, others feel their value is mainly aesthetic. In fact, plants play several roles: aesthetics, odour and insect control and, to a greater or lesser extent, facilitating waste-water treatment (see Table 9.3). Let's examine each function in more detail.

The aesthetic role of wetland plants is an important one, but often underrated. The pleasant appearance of constructed wetlands has attracted many people to the idea of ecological sewage treatment. They improve the appearance of neighbourhoods and provide a habitat for wildlife. Many constructed wetlands double as public recreation areas and attract hikers, joggers and birdwatchers. The plants and the layer of litter they form help to control odours by creating a natural biofilter. This makes wetlands much more pleasant and acceptable to neighbouring communities. They also choke out weeds and prevent too many insects from breeding on the water surface. As far as their role in waste-water treatment is concerned, aquatic plants provide a large

Table 9.3 *Relative Importance of Plants in Different Constructed Wetland Designs*

Attribute	Surface flow	Horizontal flow	Vertical flow	Combined
Stabilize surface	*****	*****	***	***
Reduce flow velocity	***	–	–	–
Attenuate light	*****	**	*	***
Insulation	***	***	***	***
Attached microbes	*****	***	*	*
Uptake of nutrients	*****	*	–	*
Oxygen transfer/release	*	**	*	*
Wildlife habitat	*****	***	*	*
Aesthetics	*****	*****	***	*****

Key: Number of stars increases with importance of process. A dash indicates that a process has no importance.
Source: Brix (1994)

surface area for the bacteria that break down organic pollutants. The root systems stabilize the surface of the soil and prevent the formation of erosion channels. In surface flow systems the vegetation reduces the water current velocity and thereby creates better conditions for the sedimentation of suspended solids. Plants provide insulation in the winter and help to keep the underlying substrate free of frost. How much the metabolism of these plants affects the treatment processes depends on design. They do filter the waste-water physically, and some species take up metals. It is often claimed that certain aquatic plants, such as common reeds and cattails, provide oxygen via their root zones by virtue of their hollow stems. In practice, research has shown that the amount of oxygen that can reliably be expected to be released by the plants is nominal in most vertical flow systems, and limited to the immediate environment around the roots.

Waste Stabilization Ponds

Waste stabilization ponds, also known as sewage lagoons or oxidation ponds, are one of the oldest and most widely-used waste-water treatment systems, particularly in the US. Essentially these are shallow ponds, 1–1.5 metres deep, often linked together in a series. They contain bacteria, green and blue algae and small invertebrates, and often higher plants and fish as well.

Ponds treat waste-water through a variety of aerobic and anaerobic processes. Essentially, there are two layers to the pond. The top layer is aerobic. Oxygen diffuses from the air into the water at the surface, and the action of wind encourages additional aeration. Algae also produce oxygen in the presence of sunlight, through the process of photosynthesis. In contrast, the bottom layer of the pond is anaerobic.

In the top layer, aerobic bacteria break down organic material into nutrients and carbon dioxide. These end products are subsequently taken up by algae, fuelling the process of photosynthesis. Suspended solids settle to the bottom layer of the pond, where anaerobic bacteria digest them, significantly reducing their volume. Because the anaerobic layer is covered by an aerobic layer, odours from anaerobic digestion are not a big problem.

Incoming water is directed towards the bottom of the first pond, which is often deeper than subsequent ponds to encourage anaerobic digestion. Waste-water stays in each pond for 1–3 weeks. In later ponds, where the waste-water has been substantially cleansed, fish and water lilies can thrive, reducing the level of algae. Reeds, cattails and rushes are often planted around the edge of each pond, creating small wetland areas and contributing to the cleansing process.

A multiple pond system can provide full primary and secondary treatment, or even tertiary treatment, reducing BOD by 97 per cent and pathogens by more than 95 per cent. Organic nitrogen is mineralized to ammonia, which then undergoes volatilization, nitrification/denitrification or microbial assimilation. Phosphates are taken up by plants and algae, or precipitate out. Pond systems are inherently robust, because any sudden dose of pollutants is diluted in the large volume of water.

Ponds offer the advantage of being cheap and easy to construct, and very simple to maintain. On average, 10 square metres of pond is required to treat the waste of one person.

Floating Aquatic Plant Systems

Floating aquatic plant systems use plants such as water hyacinths or duckweed to treat waste-water. They were orginally developed as an improvement on sewage lagoons.

Water Hyacinth Systems

The floating aquatic plant system was born when researchers tried adding water hyacinths (*Eichornia crassipes*) to traditional waste stabilization ponds to produce cleaner water and reduce odours (see Figure 9.3). The result was a system that could provide tertiary treatment in less than half the time it takes an ordinary lagoon system to provide secondary treatment. Water hyacinth systems work rather differently. Treatment in a hyacinth system occurs in three ways: the suspended solids settle to the bottom, the plants take up nitrogen and (to a lesser extent) phosphorus, and microbes living on the hyacinth roots transform nitrogen to ammonia through nitrification/denitrification. Phosphate uptake appears to be limited to 50–70 per cent, even if the plants are routinely harvested (see Table 9.4).

Hyacinths are particularly good at taking up trace metals (see Table 9.5). For example, they have been used to remove metals from photoprocessing waste-water. Analysis of the plant tissue reveals metal concentrations hundreds to thousands of times those in water or sediments. Hyacinth systems can be designed for treatment of raw waste-water, primary effluent, upgrading of existing secondary treatment systems, or advanced secondary or even tertiary treatment. The retention time varies between 5 and 15 days, and the hyacinths must be harvested periodically; they can be used as a fertilizer and soil conditioner, or as an animal feed supplement. The biggest drawback to the water hyacinth system is the fact that the hyacinths are highly susceptible to frost, making the systems viable only in the tropics and subtropics, or within a heated greenhouse in colder climates. However, there are several other floating aquatic plants that are frost-tolerant, including watercress, European iris and duckweed.

DUCKWEED SYSTEMS

Duckweeds (*Lemna*, *Spirodella* and *Wolffia*) are the smallest and the simplest of the flowering plants. They also have one of the fastest reproduction rates – a single plant can double its weight in

Table 9.4 *Performance of Hyacinth Waste-water Treatment Systems (Percentage Removal)*

Location	BOD	Suspended solids	Total nitrogen	Total phosphorus
National Space Tech. Lab., MS	93.6	89.7	71.7	56.8
Lucedale MS	85.7	95.2	NA	NA
Orange Grove MS	72.0	69.4	NA	NA
Williamson Cr., TX	87.0	91.2	57.1	18.6
Coral Springs FL	23.1	NA	95.5	67.3

NA = not available
Source: Reed *et al.* (1995)

111

Table 9.5 *Metal Removal in Hyacinth Ponds*

Metal	Influent concentration (per litre)	Percentage removal
Boron	0.14 milligrams	37
Copper	27.6 grams	20
Iron	457.8 grams	34
Manganese	18.2 grams	37
Lead	12.8 grams	68
Cadmium	0.4 grams	46
Chromium	0.8 grams	22
Arsenic	0.9 grams	18

Note: systems have an average of three parallel channels and a detention time of approximately 5 days
Source: Reed *et al.* (1995)

18 hours. Recently, researchers have begun to investigate their potential for waste-water treatment.

Duckweeds absorb nitrogen, phosphorus and heavy metals, and they remove 90–95 per cent of BOD and suspended solids. Much of the nitrogen and phosphorus is taken up by the plants, which must be harvested to ensure the system continues to work effectively. Because they form such a dense mat on the water surface, duckweeds offer the additional advantage of eliminating mosquito problems. And unlike water hyacinths, they will grow in temperatures as low as 1–3°C.

In 1992 there were at least 15 operational waste-water treat-

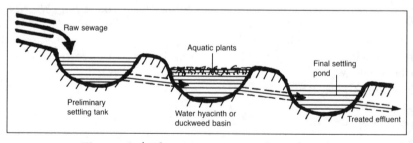

Figure 9.4 *Floating Aquatic Plant System*

ment facilities in the US that used duckweed, including a system at Del Monte's food processing plant in Minnesota to clean its industrial waste-water to discharge standards. The greatest weakness of floating aquatic plant systems is their reliance on one or just a few plant species. This leaves them vulnerable – if anything kills off that species, the system will no longer function.

Combined Systems

Systems that combine different treatment processes are growing in popularity. They offer greater control over the cleansing process than a single-unit system where all the processes happen at the same time and within the same space. There are hundreds of possible designs that can be used, but two are particularly popular: the marsh-pond-meadow multistage system used in the US, and the Max-Planck-Institute Process used in Europe.

The marsh-pond-meadow system comprises five steps: (1) initial screening of the incoming waste-water followed by aeration; (2) a surface flow marsh planted with cattails in a sand medium; (3) a pond with aquatic plants and fish; (4) a meadow planted with reed canary grass; and (5) a chlorination chamber to provide final disinfection. The system can remove 77 per cent of nitrogen in the form of ammonia and 82 per cent of total phosphorus.

The Max-Planck-Institute Process was developed in France. It consists of four or five stages in cascade, each with several basins laid out in parallel. The first two stages are surface flow beds, which are loaded alternately, followed by subsurface flow beds. Suspended solid and BOD removal are good, but the system is not as efficient at removing nitrogen and phosphorus.

Living Machine Systems

Living machine treatment is the brainchild of John Todd, a Canadian-born marine biologist. He based his philosophy of waste-water treatment on the premise that it must be possible to purify water 'as nature does', using energy from the sun and ecosystems comprising a rich variety of organisms that obtain their energy,

---

Box 9.1 Camphill Village Waste-water Treatment Systems at Oaklands Park

The Camphill Village systems at Oaklands Park in Gloucestershire, England, are variations of the Max-Planck-Institute Process. Their success has attracted the attention of the UK waste-water industry.

There are two separate systems at Oaklands Park, one treating domestic sewage from a population of 35, the other from a population of 65. In System 1, a septic tank provides preliminary and primary level treatment; in System 2, a settlement tank is used instead. In both systems, secondary treatment is provided by two sets of constructed wetlands, a pond, flowforms, more constructed wetlands and a final lagoon.

The first set of wetlands are vertical flow beds planted with common reeds. They operate in parallel on a cycle of 2 days on, 10 days off. Next is a second set of parallel subsurface flow wetlands. These are planted with *Phragmites, Scirpus lacustris* and *Iris pseudacorus*, and they operate on a cycle of 4 days on, 8 days off. The small stilling pond settles out humus and acts as a recycling basin for the flowforms which follow. The flowforms are symmetrical sculpted basins that impart rhythmical, natural movements to the water and encourage aeration.

Water then flows into the third set of wetlands. These can be switched from vertical flow mode to horizontal flow mode. They are planted with a greater variety of species than the previous beds: *Scirpus lacustris, Iris pseudacorus, Spargnum, Acorus calamus* and *Carexelata*. The final lagoon is a shallow pond edged with a variety of plants and stocked with carp, goldfish, bream and rudd.

The systems perform well. They remove 98 per cent of BOD and suspended solids and create a fully nitrified effluent that meets European Union bathing water standards. Phosphorous is also reduced: by 23 per cent in System 1 and 68 per cent in System 2. The cost per capita for design and construction was roughly £325.

Source: Burke and Lawrence (1990)

---

directly or indirectly, from the sun. In 1980, he founded a research organization, Ocean Arks International, to explore the potential for solar-based waste-water treatment, among other things. The research was sufficiently promising that in 1988 a business arm of the company – Environmental Engineering Associates (EEA) – was created to promote and establish living machine waste-water treatment systems.

How It Works

Living machine systems combine aquaculture and constructed wetland systems and enclose them in a greenhouse to create a highly efficient waste-water treatment process. In doing so, they eliminate three of the biggest drawbacks to natural treatment systems: the large areas of land required, the long retention periods required, and their suboptimal performance in cold weather.

Each living machine system is different, designed specifically for each individual situation, but a typical system works something like this (see Figure 9.4). Incoming waste-water is screened and degritted. It then goes to tanks where it is mixed and aerated, keeping the solids in suspension. Next, it is separated into several streams and directed into a series of translucent tanks filled with plants, algae and snails. In these tanks, a number of things happen. Microbes that live on the roots of the floating plants break down organic matter in the waste-water and degrade contaminants. They also convert ammonia to nitrogen, which is subsequently taken up by the algae. The plants take up heavy metals, phosphorus and nitrogen, while the algae also take up phosphorus and release oxygen. Snails feed on the algae and suspended organic particles.

The next stage comprises constructed wetlands, which polish the water from the tanks and remove nitrates. The oxygenless environment of the marsh reduces nitrates to nitrogen gas. Any remaining phosphorus is taken up by plants or adsorbed to the substrate. Pathogenic bacteria are killed by the cattails, irises and bulrushes in the marsh, which exude antimicrobial chemicals. The bulrushes and reeds absorb any remaining organic and inorganic material, while any remaining suspended solids settle out. Finally, the treated waste-water is disinfected with ultraviolet radiation.

Living machine systems are probably best suited to urban areas where land is at a premium. Their construction and operation costs are high compared with constructed wetlands or soil-based systems – a living machine system designed to treat the waste of 330 people at Findhorn, Scotland cost £160,000 to build, and the electricity costs to run the pumps totals £4000 each year.

Thus they are best compared with conventional treatment systems in urban areas, and here they offer several advantages. They cost roughly two-thirds as much to build as a conventional treatment system, and their running costs are much less, as they draw a

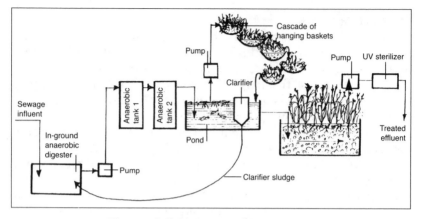

Figure 9.5 *Living Machine System*

lot of energy from the sun and they do not require the use of chemicals. Operating costs for a module that treats 180 cubic metres a day are approximately US$25,000 per year, and there is the possibility of revenue from sales of cut flowers and decorative plants. They produce less sludge, avoiding much of the headache of sludge disposal that conventional systems face. And, of course, they are much more pleasant to look at (and to smell) than a conventional sewage treatment plant.

It should be noted that living machine technology is much less widely used, and has been tested far less, than constructed wetland technology or soil-based treatment systems. There have been very few scientific papers written on the subject, and thus much of the information in this section comes from articles in industry publications rather than peer-reviewed journals, and should be viewed with a certain degree of skepticism. Because there are relatively few systems in operation, it is not possible to provide 'average' figures on the performance of living machine systems. What follows, therefore, are case histories of two of the older and better documented systems.

SUGARBUSH

The first pilot living machine system was installed at a ski resort in Vermont in 1987. The lagoon system in place at the time was frequently failing to meet discharge regulations, and the resort owners were looking for an effective, reliable system. It was a challenging trial project to undertake. The regulations for discharging to the small brook that crossed the leachfield were extremely strict in order to protect the trout that inhabited it. Furthermore, the demands placed on the system fluctuated dramatically, from a population of a few hundred people during the summer to several thousand on weekends during the peak skiing season. Finally, the system had to perform in subzero temperatures.

EEA installed a 57 cubic metre system comprising nine translucent tanks, a raceway and a wetland section. Waste-water flowed through the first three tanks, into the raceway, through the final six tanks, and then through the wetland. The tanks contained algae that took up nutrients, and bacteria that began digesting the organic material and nitrifying the ammonia. The raceways were filled with willows, duckweed, umbrella plants, cypresses, purple loosestrife and eucalyptus trees and were populated with bacteria, algae and zooplankton. Tiny freshwater shrimp fed on the algae and the sludge. The final wetland section was filled with gravel and planted with cattails, bulrushes and reeds. It took approximately 13 days for waste-water to pass through the system. The results were mixed. The system was highly effective at removing BOD and suspended solids, but it did not consistently meet the discharge requirements for ammonia and phosphorus (see Table 9.6).

Table 9.6 *Sugarbush Average Performance Data for January 1988 to March 1989*

Constituent	Influent (milligrams per litre)	Effluent (milligrams per litre)	Percentage removed
BOD	220	10	96
Suspended solids	162	6	96
Organic nitrogen	29	4	86
Ammonia	22	8	64
Nitrate	0.6	9	–
Dissolved phosphorus	5	5	0
Faecal coliforms	6×10^6/100 millilitres	1500	>99

Source: Reed (1992)

Although it attracted a lot of interest and became a tourist draw, ultimately it was not chosen because it failed to meet the strict ammonia regulations consistently.

HARWICH

However, the Sugarbush system was successful enough for the town of Harwich on Cape Cod to ask EEA to design a pilot plant to treat their septage. Septage is the concentrated liquid pumped out of septic tanks; it is 10–20 times more concentrated than municipal sewage. Cape Cod had an increasingly serious problem of liquids leaching out of septic tanks and contaminating the ground-water, and they were looking for a low cost, ecologically sound solution.

The living machine pilot project consisted of a 13 by 39 metre greenhouse containing four parallel rows of transparent tanks and constructed marshes. It treated 4.5 cubic metres of septage a day, and it took 12 days for the septage to pass through the system. The treated effluent that came out of the other end was dramatically cleaner. Nitrates were reduced well below drinking-water standards, while BOD and suspended solids were almost entirely eliminated (see Table 9.7). Fish living at the end of the system were analysed for PCBs, dioxins and other contaminants; none were found. The success of the initial project convinced Harwich to fund a permanent system, which began operation in 1990. It also won John Todd a merit award from the EPA.

Table 9.7 *Harwich Data: First 6 Months of Operation*

Constituent	Influent (milligrams per litre)	Effluent (milligrams per litre)	Percentage removed
BOD	1296	5.3	99.6
Suspended solids	421	5.4	98.7
Total nitrogen	164	12.8	92.2
Total phosphorus	28	9.6	65.7

Source: Spencer (1990)

OTHER PROJECTS

Since then, many more living machine systems have been built: in the US, in Canada and, recently, in the UK. Some treat sewage and septage, others tackle industrial and commerical waste. For example, a system in Vermont treats dairy waste from Ben & Jerry's ice cream plant. A pilot project to treat waste from a fertilizer manufacturing plant has recently been installed in Alberta, and a system is in place at the Body Shop's Canadian headquarters in Toronto, initially to deal with its non-industrial waste, but ultimately to treat the waste from the manufacturing processes.

Chapter 10

Coda: Rethinking Water Carriage

'The land impoverished and the water infected'

(Victor Hugo)

The adoption of water carriage in the nineteenth century had several major impacts. Foremost amongst these was that it promoted the attitude that watercourses are acceptable dumping grounds for our wastes – an attitude that persists today. There were other impacts as well. Large public works require lots of money: sanitary sewers and sewage treatment plants are capital-intensive undertakings. This meant that sewage disposal became a municipal responsibility rather than the individual responsibility of private citizens. Not only have we given up responsibility for treating our waste, we no longer even know what happens to it. As modern sewage treatment has become increasingly centralized in the name of economy of scale, we have become increasingly detached from the treatment process. This ignorance has allowed wide-scale water pollution to occur. We assume sewage treatment plants can remove anything we flush away, while in reality there are many dangerous and toxic chemicals they cannot treat.

Water carriage has also changed our attitudes towards human waste. Today we no longer see sewage as a potential resource that can be used as fertilizer or compost; we see it only as a potentially dangerous waste that should be removed as quickly as possible. Perhaps most importantly, water carriage has created a tremendous ecological imbalance. The food we consume comes from the land. In the natural course of events, we would return our waste to the land, enriching the soil with nutrients and organic matter, enabling it to produce more food. Instead we take those valuable nutrients and organic matter and dump them in the water, where they create pollution. Then we need to use chemical fertilizers to restore the productivity of the depleted soil.

COMPOSTING TOILETS

Using water to flush away faeces and urine is one of the biggest contributors to water pollution. It is also a tremendous waste of water, an increasingly valuable and scarce resource. Instead of trying to develop more and more effective ways to take organic waste out of the sewage-contaminated water that arrives at a sewage treatment plant, perhaps it's time to reconsider the whole idea of water carriage. According to ecological engineer Greg Allen, 'Waste doesn't exist in nature. What is discarded by one is the food of another. What we are doing by discarding our faeces into the ocean is, in effect, mining the soils, denying them the return of that nutrient, and soiling our waters in the process' (Allen, 1993). What is the alternative? The most attractive answer is a composting toilet which involves no water whatsoever. Now, most of us don't consider composting toilets an attractive answer, because we associate them with malodorous pit privies or outhouses. This is an unfortunate and inaccurate comparison, because composting toilets are actually quite different. A pit privy is anaerobic; the organic matter falls into a heap that gets packed down as more material falls on top, so oxygen can't penetrate. When organic matter decomposes anaerobically, it produces methane and hydrogen sulphide gases, which are responsible for the offensive odours. In contrast, composting toilets create an aerobic environment, and organic matter that breaks down aerobically produces odourless carbon dioxide and water.

The principle is simple. Composting toilets collect faeces, urine, toilet paper (and sometimes kitchen waste as well) in an aerated container, where bacteria and other microorganisms are ready to go to work. They decompose the waste, reducing the volume by as much as 90 per cent, and leave a humus-like residue. To do this successfully, they must have good aeration, sufficient moisture, and an ambient temperature of at least 15°C. Ideally, the carbon-to-nitrogen ratio should be 30:1. All a good composting toilet needs to do is create and maintain these conditions.

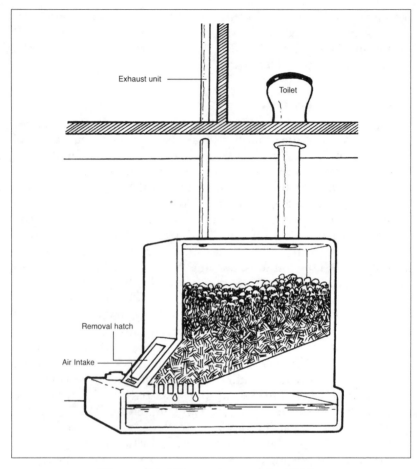

Figure 10.1 *Large Composting Toilet*

The first self-contained, indoor composting toilet was developed in Sweden in 1939. This model was later named the Clivus Multrum, and it remains one of the most popular commercial systems. Although composting toilets achieved moderate success in Scandinavia, they had limited success elsewhere. In the 1970s there were murmurs of interest in the US: a few commercial models were installed in national parks and the back-to-the-land movement experimented with do-it-yourself designs. Today the do-it-yourself designs have been improved, and there are a growing number of commercial composting toilet systems available.

Commercial designs fall into two basic categories. The first is a relatively large, expensive unit that requires little maintenance, is emptied only once every few years and has few moving parts (see Figure 10.1). Because the tank is so big, it must be put in the basement. Large models achieve a good ambient temperature simply through the mass of organic material they collect in the tank; as the organic material at the core of the pile breaks down, it generates heat, while the material surrounding the core provides insulation. Aeration is achieved through an intake vent near the bottom of the tank and a vent pipe at the top. As air in the tank is warmed by the decomposing organic material, it rises, escaping out of the top of the pipe. This creates a partial vacuum within the composting tank, drawing air from the intake vent through the wastes, which keeps everything aerobic. The vent pipe also eliminates odours, and the partial vacuum prevents odours from reaching the bathroom when the toilet seat is up by creating a slight down draught.

Some of the newer commercial models feature 'batch composting', rather than the more common 'continuous composting'. This means the toilets have more than one composting chamber. As one fills up with fresh waste, the others are left to mature undisrupted.

The other design is a smaller, less expensive unit, roughly half the price of a large unit. It includes a heater, a fan and possibly an automatic mixing unit, and is small enough to fit in most bathrooms (see Figure 10.2). Because there is not enough organic mass in a small unit to generate sufficient heat, a low temperature electric heater is necessary to keep the tank warm enough for effective bacterial action. The fan in the vent pipe keeps the tank aerobic by drawing air through the contents, and it prevents odours from emerging when the lid over the seat is raised. Some units have an internal device for stirring and aerating the wastes, usually operated by a handle projecting outside the unit. A small model must be emptied at least once a year.

There are also a number of home-built models. The most efficient design that requires the least maintenance is probably the twin vault composting privy (see Figure 10.3). Essentially, this is a box divided into two compartments. The toilet seat can be moved from the top of one compartment to the top of the other. Faeces

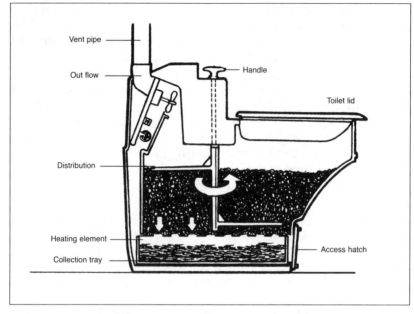

Figure 10.2 *Small Composting Toilet*

and urine fall directly into the compartment below, and a little 'soak' (sawdust, ash, etc.) is added after each use to achieve the proper moisture content and a good carbon-to-nitrogen ratio.

The compartments are aerated in a similar manner to the large commercial models: air in the compartment is warmed by the decomposing organic matter and escapes up a flue. This creates a partial vacuum that pulls air through screened vents in the access panels and into the organic mass. When one compartment becomes full, the seat is moved to sit on top of the other chamber, and the contents of the first are left alone to decompose for roughly a year, by which time the other compartment is full. The finished compost is removed via the access panel.

The finished product is a humus-like substance that is 10–20 per cent of the original volume. It can be used in the garden like ordinary compost, with the caveat that, although the risk of contracting a disease from this composted waste is extremely low, it is safest not to apply it on edible plants.

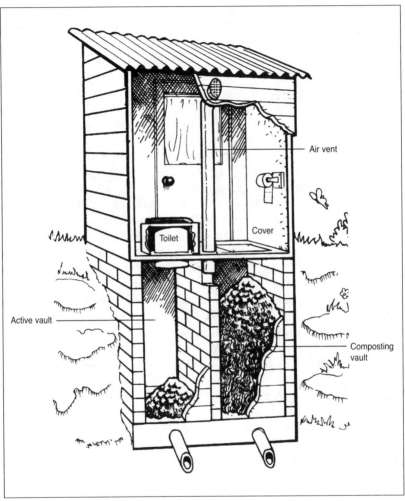

Air vent

Cover

Toilet

Active vault

Composting vault

Figure 10.3 *Twin Vault Composting Privy*

Composting toilets are far superior to flush toilets in terms of ecological impact, but they do have a few disadvantages. Foremost among these, in a society accustomed to the flush toilet, is the psychological barrier to composting human waste. Composting toilets also demand some patience and tolerance to deal with the problems that may arise. 'To own and use a composting toilet requires a commitment to recycle human waste, at least a minimal amount of maintenance, and a basic understanding of the biological processes by which organic materials degrade', David Riggle writes (1996). Some companies now offer a service contract with their commercial models, so owners don't have to worry about maintenance.

However, operating a composting toilet may present a few hazards. First of all, it can take some time for the composting system to stabilize, and during this initial phase odours can be a problem. Flies can be an ongoing problem: they prosper in the welcoming environment of the tank. A well designed vent pipe with a fine-mesh fly-screen will help, but the sparing use of biodegradable insecticides may be necessary. Finally, there can be problems of undersupply or oversupply, particularly in small composting toilets. Going away for a few weeks' holiday may upset the balance, as may a large party with plenty of beer. There may also be external problems to grapple with. Unfortunately, in many areas, local plumbing codes exclude composting toilets from consideration, or permit them only as an additional toilet in a household already equipped with a flush toilet. It can take patience and persistence to overcome these regulatory hurdles.

Currently, composting toilets are most commonly used in remote areas that are not connected to the mains, where the site is not suitable for a septic tank and leachfield, or where water is in short supply. However, there is also a growing interest in using them in urban areas as an 'environmentally friendly' alternative to water carriage. There are many instances of composting toilets in private homes, and even in larger buildings. For example, at Canada's University of British Columbia, a 9000 square metre office complex is serviced entirely by composting toilets.

Grey-water Systems

If you use a composting toilet with the goal of becoming independent of sewer mains, you are still left with the problem of what to do with 'grey-water' – the used water from bathtubs, showers, sinks and laundry machines. This is best treated in some form of constructed wetland. The biggest challenge in treating household grey-water is dealing with the quantity of soap, grease and food wastes.

This can be as demanding to treat as sewage effluent. There are several options for treatment: for example, subsurface or overland irrigation, constructed wetlands, or membrane filter technology. It is the waste-water from the kitchen sink, containing grease, soap and food waste, that presents the biggest treatment challenge.

Part IV

Ground-water

Chapter 11

Ground-water: The Special Issues

Ground-water has several unique characteristics that make ground-water pollution a particular challenge to clean up. Ground-water is formed when rain-water percolates through the soil and into underground reserves called aquifers. These occur in layers of rocks such as sandstone or gravel that are porous and permeable enough to store water and let it flow through them easily, or in fractured rock such as granite or basalt. Once in the aquifers, ground-water can remain there for tens to thousands of years before eventually making its way out and into streams, rivers, lakes and oceans.

Many of the cleansing processes that occur in surface-water do not take place underground. Ground-water is not exposed to air or sunlight, which help to break down organic compounds, and because the contaminants are trapped underground, volatile compounds cannot evaporate. The long residence time means pollutants are not flushed out, nor is there a lot of clean, incoming water to dilute the pollutants. Furthermore, aquifers have fewer of the microorganisms that break down organic contaminants in surface-water. Finally, contaminants can become trapped in inaccessible nooks and crannies of the aquifer and adsorb to the surface of the rocks, creating a long-term source of pollution within the aquifer. For all these reasons, contaminants in ground-water can be far more concentrated than in surface-water and persist for much longer.

Many areas rely on ground-water for their drinking-water supplies. If aquifers become polluted for any reason, the ground-water can become undrinkable, and nearby surface water can also be contaminated as the polluted ground-water migrates out of the aquifer. There are thousands of cases of localized pollution contaminating drinking supplies. In Coventry, England, for example, where ground-water supplies a quarter of the city's drinking water needs, a European Union study found nearly all the boreholes had total solvent concentrations of more than 10 micrograms per litre. Even more common are cases where shallow wells in rural areas become contaminated by agricultural chemicals or bacteria from leaking septic tanks. Ground-water can become contaminated in a number of ways: leaching of nitrates from fertilizers and manure, leaching of pesticides, accidental spills, illegal dumping, mining activity, leaking landfill sites and underground storage tanks, and salt-water intrusion in coastal areas caused by withdrawing too much fresh water from aquifers.

The extent of the problem is difficult to gauge. In Europe, few data are available – traditionally ground-water is not monitored as much as surface-water. In the US, the EPA estimates there are 300,000–400,000 contaminated sites with a combined clean-up bill of more than US$750 billion. Whatever the current situation, it is safe to guess the problem will worsen in the future. Because it takes a long time for contaminants to percolate through the soil to aquifers, the pollution we're dealing with today was actually created several decades ago. In the meantime, agriculture has intensified, so more and more fertilizers and pesticides are being used, and the excess is slowly making its way towards underground aquifers.

Sources of Pollution

LEAKING LANDFILL SITES AND UNDERGROUND STORAGE TANKS

Municipal landfills, industrial waste disposal sites and leaking underground storage tanks are the most significant point sources of ground-water pollution. They are particularly dangerous if they are sited near sand and gravel aquifers, because contaminants can percolate readily through these substrates and into the underlying aquifers.

Until relatively recently, landfill sites were not lined; trash was thrown into abandoned quarries or pits dug into the ground and then covered over with a layer of soil. In these conditions, there is nothing to prevent rain-water from infiltrating the site and causing contaminants to leach into ground-water. Many countries now insist that all landfill sites be lined and equipped with trenches to intercept any leachate, but even these sites have been known to leak. In the US, a study by the EPA found 74 per cent of designated hazardous waste sites had leaked and contaminated ground-water with heavy metals and organic solvents. In the UK, the Department of the Environment found one third of landfill sites analysed had contaminated ground-water or surface-water. What is particularly worrying about leaking landfill sites is that most towns obtain their ground-water and dispose of their landfill in the same general area, calling into question the quality of the drinking water.

Leaking underground storage tanks are another extremely common problem. Underground storage tanks are used by service stations to store petrol, and by various industries to store all kinds of oils, chemicals and wastes. For many years these tanks were routinely made of steel. Unfortunately, steel corrodes, and by the time a steel tank is 15 years old, there is a 50 per cent chance it will leak.

Large numbers of these tanks were installed in the 1950s and 1960s. Four decades later, leaking tanks are a major headache. For example, a recent EPA survey found 35 per cent of motor fuel storage tanks leaked. Today fibreglass tanks are being used to replace the corroded steel ones. They are more reliable and not prone to corrosion, although they are more likely to crack.

AGRICULTURAL CHEMICALS

When pesticide use first became popular with farmers, the scientific community believed that these chemicals were not a threat to ground-water. Pesticides that were not taken up by plants would become immobilized in the upper soil levels, they said, or would break down before reaching ground-water. This proved to be wishful thinking.

Modern, chemically intensive methods of agriculture are responsible for an increasing proportion of ground-water contamination. Recent studies show that the levels of pesticides and nitrates in ground-water are a matter for concern. It now appears that pesticides can migrate into the water table, and even short-lived, unstable compounds can become extremely tenacious once they move below the biologically active soil zone. They percolate particularly quickly through sandy soils and chalk.

Worldwide, there is no clear picture of the nature or extent of pesticide contamination. Most countries do not routinely analyse ground-water for pesticides – there are too many to test for, and the chemical analysis is expensive. However, it is easy to pinpoint areas that are vulnerable to contamination: areas where intensive agriculture occurs in coarse soil, low in organic matter, on top of unconfined aquifers, such as in Denmark, northern France, the Netherlands, Lithuania and Belarus. It is also unclear how great a threat this is to human health. There is no consensus on what constitutes a safe level of pesticides in drinking water: the European Union sets a standard of 0.1 micrograms per litre for individual pesticides, but the World Health Organization and the US EPA permit 20–30 times that level. Even with their laxer standards, the EPA estimates that 1 per cent of drinking water wells in the US exceed safe limits for pesticides.

Intensive agricultural practices also involve the use of lots of manure and artificial fertilizers. This has led to nitrate leaching, and, to a lesser extent, to phosphorus leaching. A large proportion of the nutrients applied to crops is not actually taken up by the plants; some gets washed off with surface runoff, and the remainder percolates into the soil.

In the case of nitrogen, the portion that percolates into the soil is converted into soluble nitrates by microorganisms. These nitrates can leach below the root zone and eventually into the ground-water, creating health risks if the aquifer is a source of drinking-water. Nitrates in drinking-water can cause 'blue baby' syndrome, a condition where an infant's red blood cells can't carry enough oxygen to the body. Laboratory research suggests nitrates may also be linked to stomach cancer, but the epidemiological evidence for this is weak. Nitrate pollution is a problem in areas where intensive agriculture occurs in sandy soils on top of unconsolidated, unconfined aquifers: north-western Europe, the Czech Republic, the Slovak Republic, Hungary, the Ukraine and Belarus. Estimates suggest that the ground-water in over 85 per cent of agricultural areas in Europe has nitrate concentrations that exceed the guide level of 25 milligrams per litre.

ACIDIFICATION
When the pH of a body of water drops too much, the water becomes undrinkable. Metals such as aluminium dissolve more readily in acidic water, making it toxic. So, for example, if drinking-water is too acidic, it will leach metals from pipes in the distribution system. This is not good for human health, nor is it good for the distribution system.

There is not much information on the global extent of ground-water acidification, but it is well established that soil acidification is a serious problem in much of Europe. Because water filters through the soil before it reaches underground aquifers, it is likely that ground-water is becoming acidified where it lies below sandy, poorly buffered soils in areas of acid rain. Ground-water acidification has been documented in Denmark, and it is estimated that if the trend continues, the ground-water in western Denmark will become sufficiently acidic that it will be unfit for human consumption without expensive treatment.

SALINIZATION
The best documented source of ground-water contamination is probably salinization. This problem occurs in coastal areas where too much fresh water is withdrawn from the aquifers. As the aquifer becomes depleted, salt-water rushes in to fill it up, making the ground-water unfit for drinking. It is a problem in many areas: in England, in aquifers near the Mersey, Humber and Thames estuaries; in Canada, on Prince Edward Island; and in Europe, in coastal regions of the Mediterranean, the Baltic and the Black Sea, to name a few.

To date, there is no cost-effective way to reverse this. Salinization can be prevented by reducing water withdrawal from coastal aquifers, or by drilling strategic wells and pumping them to prevent salt-water from reaching the depleted aquifers.

MINING AND INDUSTRIAL WASTES
Finally, mining and industrial wastes are also common sources of ground-water pollution. This category includes a slew of contaminants: heavy metals, salts, arsenic, polyaromatic hydrocarbons, oil

products and synthetic organic compounds. There are numerous examples. On Canada's east coast, leachates from abandoned gold mines have contaminated ground-water supplies with arsenic, while in Europe, mining has contaminated between 15,000 and 30,000 square kilometres of ground-water. In California's Silicon Valley, the ground-water is so laden with toxics that it may never be able to be used for drinking. In the UK, hundreds of water supply boreholes have become contaminated with solvents, making them unfit for consumption.

Ground-water Treatment

To date, ground-water remediation has proved to be an expensive and often fruitless exercise. The US government has committed billions of dollars to clean up contaminated aquifers to drinking-water standards, but a decade of experience suggests this is simply not possible in many cases. On an encouraging note, the federal funding has stimulated a lot of research into ground-water remediation, and the technologies that are emerging have improved our ability to clean up contaminated aquifers.

There are a number of approaches to ground-water remediation. When pollutants reach an underground aquifer, they create a contaminated 'plume' of ground-water that can travel through the aquifer. Some remediation methods focus on preventing or minimizing pollutant movement into ground-water, or on preventing the contaminated plume from reaching areas of clean, usable water. These techniques are referred to as 'abatement' methods. In contrast, 'restoration' methods actually attempt to clean up the pollution, usually by removing the source (or sources) of pollution and decontaminating the polluted portion of the aquifer. Both approaches are time-consuming and expensive.

ABATEMENT METHODS

Abatement methods encompass several techniques. One is the barrier method, which confines the contamination to the smallest possible area of the aquifer and contains it there indefinitely using underground walls of clay, cement or steel. Depending on the material used, these walls are driven directly into the ground, injected through holes, or installed in trenches dug into the aquifer. Once in place, these barriers require no maintenance. Another method is the interceptor system, where a trench is strategically excavated below the water table to divert the contaminated plume away from clean areas of the aquifer. These systems are relatively cheap and straightforward to install, but they are not quite as effective as other abatement techniques.

Finally, wells can be strategically drilled and then pumped to alter the direction of ground-water flow, a process sometimes referred to as plume management. The pumping must continue until all contaminants are gone. This can be a long process, with the risk that contaminants can become adsorbed to rocks within the aquifer and redissolve later. So although the water can appear clean after initial remediation, the pollutant may reappear several years down the road. Because the wells must be pumped constantly to be effective, the operation and maintenance costs of these systems are high.

RESTORATION TECHNIQUES

Restoring ground-water to its original level of purity can be done in two different ways: one is to treat the ground-water 'in situ'; that is, within the aquifer; the other is to pump out the ground-water and treat it at the surface.

In Situ Treatment Techniques

In situ treatment techniques involve adding materials to the aquifer, either chemical or biological. This approach is still relatively new, but it has attracted a lot of research attention, and the number of applications is increasing. The chemical techniques attempt to immobilize the contaminants through some kind of chemical reaction. They do not actually remove the contaminants, they merely prevent them from redissolving in the ground-water. Chemical reactions are most commonly used to neutralize and/or precipitate inorganic compounds.

In contrast, biological techniques use microorganisms to break down the contaminant into harmless compounds. They exploit the fact that bacteria feed on organic molecules, breaking them down in order to obtain energy. In the process, they convert complex molecules into simpler molecules and ultimately into water and either carbon dioxide or methane.

The challenge is to ensure that there are sufficient numbers of bacteria to break down a particular contaminant and suitable conditions for them to thrive. There are several ways to do this. Often the simplest solution is to enhance the growth of the existing soil and ground-water bacteria on the site by providing them with optimal conditions. Alternatively, engineers can harvest indigenous bacteria from the site and put them in above-ground reactors, where they can quickly grow large numbers. Finally, and most controversially, commercially produced non-native bacteria can be used. These bacteria are grown in commercial laboratories and are genetically designed to break down specific contaminants. There are many concerns about the adverse effects of spreading trillions of non-native microorganisms into a natural environment.

Whatever the source of the bacteria, the microorganisms will work most effectively if they have sufficient oxygen, moisture and nutrients (such as nitrogen and phosphorus). This may mean bubbling additional oxygen into the aquifer, or adding nitrates and phosphates. Furthermore, the pH and the temperature should be maintained in the correct range for optimal bacterial action.

There are limitations to in situ biological treatment. Some pollutants are very similar to natural compounds and bacteria will degrade them easily, while others can only be broken down through special biochemical pathways. The bacteria can be hampered by very high or very low concentrations of target chemical. They also tend to be specific to one chemical, so sites with more than one contaminant are difficult to remediate.

Currently, most in situ biological applications are used to treat petroleum hydrocarbon contamination, but there is potential for treating other organic contaminants commonly found in groundwater. Bacteria are not capable of treating inorganic contaminants.

The main advantages of in situ biological treatment are its cost-effectiveness, the fact it creates minimal disturbance to the site, and the fact that the bacteria continue to break down contaminants after the project has ended. The primary drawback is the lack of experience. While there is a wealth of information on the specific reactions that bacteria and other microorganisms can have with organic contaminants, field conditions are very different from laboratory conditions where the research is performed. There are very few installations that have been running for more than a couple of years.

Pump and Treat Techniques

The most popular ground-water clean-up technique remains the traditional 'pump and treat' approach. In this process, contaminated ground-water is removed from the aquifer and cleaned, by air stripping, carbon adsorption, chemical treatment or biological treatment. Advocates of natural systems have also suggested the contaminated water could be treated in a wetland. Once treated, the ground-water can be returned to the aquifer, or replaced by clean water.

The success rate for any type of ground-water treatment is limited. Some types of pollution are amenable to these clean-up techniques, but many are not. Often the contaminants move in unpredictable pathways, migrate to inaccessible areas of the aquifer, or adhere to subsurface materials and then redissolve later.

Even when the clean-up techniques work, they are expensive and time-consuming. A report by the US National Research Council (1992) states 'the cleanup of contaminated ground-water is inherently complex and will require large expenditures and long time periods, in some cases centuries'. Even then, restoring ground-water to drinking-water standards is not guaranteed.

Box 11.1 Ground-water Clean-up in South Brunswick Township

In 1977, toxic chlorinated solvents were discovered in one of the main wells that supplied drinking water to the New Jersey township of South Brunswick. The contaminants were traced to a nearby IBM computer manufacturing plant.

IBM agreed to clean up the site and subsequently spent US$10 million to pump and treat the ground-water. After 6 years, the aquifer was restored to drinking-water standards. However, 3 years later, the contaminant levels again exceeded drinking-water standards. While the treatment had successfully removed the dissolved contaminants, it appeared that some of the solvents had initially bound to the subsurface materials and were now re-dissolving. This case illustrates some of the limitations of traditional pump-and-treat technology.

> ### *Box 11.2 Iowa Groundwater Protection Act of 1986*
>
> Some districts have enacted specific legislation to protect ground-water. For example, the state of Iowa implemented innovative taxes to discourage ground-water pollution and fund clean-up programmes. Under the Ground-water Protection Act, Iowa taxes potential sources of ground-water contamination such as pesticides and toxic cleaning products. Wholesalers must purchase stickers for household products that produce hazardous wastes, and operators of chemical storage tanks and rubbish dumps also pay fees. The revenues are used to fund regular monitoring of wells and research into safer methods of farming.

Clearly, preventing ground-water pollution, rather than attempting to clean up the aftermath, is the best strategy. There are a number of things that must be done to achieve this. With regard to agriculture, encouraging organic practices and enacting stricter regulation and control over the use of agricultural chemicals would have far reaching effects. The problems of landfill leachate are associated with overall waste management strategies – how much waste is generated, how it is disposed of and how hazardous it is. In the short term, stricter standards for landfill management are necessary. In the longer term, we need to prevent waste generation rather than mitigate its polluting effects. Industrial pollution is a complex issue, best tackled by stricter emission laws, green taxes or tradable emission standards.

In coastal areas where salinization of aquifers is a problem, reducing the rate of water abstraction is an absolute necessity. This may be accomplished by reducing water demand, pumping in water from further inland, collecting and treating rainwater, or some combination of the above. Finally, regardless of whether these methods of preventing ground-water are pursued, we need to make bigger investments in ground-water monitoring and treatment to ensure that our drinking water supplies are safe.

Part V

Conclusions

Chapter 12

Conclusions: Directions for the Future

Pollution, according to Lord Ritchie-Calder, is the result of avarice and ignorance (Symposium on the Inter-Parliamentary Union, 1979). Avarice, because our current economic system does not take into account the costs of environmental degradation – we profit by polluting. Ignorance, because highly centralized waste-water treatment and the invisible nature of much water pollution remove us from the impact of our actions. To tackle the problem of water pollution, we need to address these underlying causes.

Our modern water carriage system has created a 'flush and forget' attitude to our wastes. We need to change that attitude. Waterways are not an appropriate dumping ground for our wastes; they cannot cope with all the toxic chemicals we have been pouring into them. Yet because most of us do not know where our wastes go and do not see the impact they have, we continue to pollute.

We need to increase the value society places on water. Clean water is vital for life, yet our economic system is not structured to reflect this fundamental truth. When we, as individuals or corporations, do not directly pay the costs of the pollution we create, either through fines or through taxation, there is little incentive to prevent or clean up our wastes, or to conserve water. Yet we all pay the price in the long term if our sources of drinking-water no longer provide drinkable water.

We need to prevent pollution. Prevention is the simplest, cheapest and most effective way to protect water resources. This means enhancing the resistence of ecosystems to pollution through watershed restoration and environmentally sensitive planning; reducing the use of toxic chemicals and recycling them whenever possible; and changing agricultural practices to reduce fertilizer and pesticide use and to prevent soil erosion.

When it comes to treating pollution, we should take a holistic approach, instead of focussing on specific pollutants or specific environmental media. We should use low technology, ecological treatment systems wherever sufficient land is available. Soil disposal techniques, constructed wetlands and living machine systems treat waste-water as well as or better than conventional treatment systems, without the need for expensive chemicals or energy.

Finally, we need to implement watershed management. It simply does not make ecological sense to manage our water resources according to political boundaries.

We have already seen increased international cooperation around issues of protecting and restoring water quality. This is not easy to accomplish, and it inevitably involves compromise, but it is a trend that must continue.

None of these recommendations is particularly new or unrealistic; they have all been implemented somewhere, in some form. Nor is it unrealistic to hope they are adopted on a wider scale. The trends are promising. Internationally, we have accepted the seriousness of water pollution, and started to make progress towards long-term, sustainable solutions. Our water quality has improved in the past two decades, and I believe it will continue to improve as ecological technologies gain ground, as the moves towards stricter emission regulations continue, and as we continue to become more aware of our impact on the environment. There is still a long way to go, but the signs are positive.

List of Terms

abatement techniques: techniques used to prevent or minimize pollutant movement into ground-water, or to prevent contaminants in ground-water from reaching areas of clean, usable water; include the use of barriers, interceptor trenches and strategic pumping

acid mine drainage: the effluent from bituminous coal mines or metal mines that contain a large concentration of acidic sulphates, including ferrous sulphate

acid rain (also known as acidic deposition or acidic precipitation): precipitation that becomes more acidic than normal (i.e. a pH lower than 5.6) after falling through polluted air and dissolving the pollutants, primarily sulphur dioxide

acidic deposition: see acid rain

acidic precipitation: see acid rain

acidification: the reduction in soil pH or the pH of a body of water

activated sludge process: a common form of secondary sewage treatment that uses aerobic bacteria in a pond or tank that is continuously aerated

adsorption: process in which a liquid or gas adheres to the outside of a solid without penetrating it

aerobic: referring to conditions or processes in which oxygen is present

algae: a group of relatively simple, mainly unicellular, aquatic plants that contain chlorophyll

ambient standards: standards that establish permissible levels of pollutants in the environment, e.g. water quality objectives

ammonia: a form of nitrogen, created as a metabolic byproduct in most animals and excreted in urine as urea or uric acid; toxic to most animal life; can be used by algae and many aquatic plants as a source of nitrogen

anaerobic: referring to conditions or processes in which oxygen is not present

aquaculture: the cultivation and harvesting of fish or shellfish

aquifer: an underground layer of porous, water-bearing sand, gravel or rock

assimilative capacity: the ability of a river or stream to disperse and break down pollutants

atmospheric deposition: deposition on land surface or in the water of pollutants that have arrived through the air, usually dissolved in rain

bioaccumulation: a process by which chemical substances are consumed and retained by organisms, either directly from the environment, or indirectly by eating food that contains the contaminants

biochemical oxygen demand (BOD): the amount of dissolved oxygen used during the decomposition of biodegradable pollutants in a sample of water

biodegradable: capable of being broken down by living organisms into inorganic compounds

biomagnification: a cumulative increase in the concentration of a persistent substance in successively higher levels of the food chain

carcinogenic: having the ability to cause cancer

catchment area: see watershed

cesspool: a large tank that collects sewage but provides no form of treatment

channelization: the practice of altering the banks of a stream or river by constructing levees, dikes, floodwalls and embankments, or straightening, widening or deepening them

chemical oxygen demand (COD): the amount of dissolved oxygen used during chemical decomposition of organic material in a sample of water

chlorinated organic compounds: see organochlorines

chlorination: a disinfection process in which chlorine is added to the treated effluent from sewage treatment plants to kill pathogens

chlororganics: see organochlorines

clinker bed: see trickling filter

closed loop cycle: a system in which pollutants in the effluent are extracted and reused as raw material

coliform bacteria: a group of bacteria normally found in the lower intestinal tract of mammals; used as an indicator of faecal contamination; includes *Escherichia coli*

combined sewer: a sewer that carries both sewage and storm-water runoff

combined sewer overflows: a point where the contents of the combined sewers are released into the environment, usually into receiving water and usually without treatment

compost toilet: a waterless toilet that creates an aerobic environment in which human waste can break down into compost

conservancy system: any sewage disposal system that returns human waste to the land

constructed wetlands: wetlands designed and built for the express purpose of treating waste-water

contaminant: any undesirable physical, chemical or biological substance in water

DDT (dichlorodiphenyltrichloroethane): an organochlorine used as an insecticide; persistent and possibly carcinogenic, banned in most developed countries

denitrification: the reduction of nitrates and nitrites to nitrogen gas by the action of denitrifying bacteria

design standards: see specification standards

digestion: a process in which complex substances are broken down into simpler compounds, either chemically or biologically

dioxin: any of a family of persistent organic compounds known chemically as polychlorinated dibenzo-p-dioxins; varying degrees of toxicity, animal carcinogen, immune suppressor, hormonal disruptor; byproduct of several industrial processes

dissolved oxygen: oxygen dissolved in water

DNA (deoxyribonucleic acid)

drainage basin: see watershed

earth closet: a waterless toilet consisting of a seat atop a bucket, which collects human waste and combines it with dry earth, charcoal or ashes from an attached hopper

effluent: sewage or industrial liquid waste released into a body of water by sewage treatment plants or industry

emission standards: see performance standards

'end-of-pipe' solutions: pollution control methods that focus on treating pollution, often from many sources, rather than preventing it

Environmental Engineering Associates (EEA)

Environmental Protection Agency (EPA)

eutrophication: a process by which lakes and ponds become enriched with dissolved nutrients, resulting in increased growth of algae and other microscopic plants; under normal conditions, it is an extremely slow process, but it is dramatically speeded up by nutrient pollution from sewage, fertilizers and runoff

externality: those costs and benefits of an economic transaction that do not accrue directly to the producer or consumer of the good or service being transacted, but are borne instead by those who are not party to the transaction

floating aquatic plant systems: waste-water treatment systems that use floating aquatic plants such as water hyacinths or duckweed

Great Lakes Water Quality Agreement (GLWQA)

heavy metals: any of a large group of metallic elements with a relatively high atomic weight, including lead, cadmium, mercury, chromium, iron and zinc; most are toxic in relatively small amounts

household hazardous waste: waste produced by consumers that poses a risk to human health or the environment humus: the organic portion of soil formed from the partial decomposition of plant or animal material

impermeable: does not permit the passage of water

in situ techniques: ground-water clean-up methods that use chemicals or bacteria to treat the contamination directly in the aquifer

integrated pest management (IPM): control of pest organisms through a mix of biological, mechanical and chemical methods; generally uses mechanical and biological means to maintain pest populations at low levels, resorting to chemicals only to control outbreaks, and then as specific to the target population as possible

integrated pollution prevention and control: a holistic approach that takes into account all pollution sources and all environmental media, and reduces the use of natural resources and energy, exposure to hazardous substances and release of pollutants

intensive agriculture: farming practices designed to increase productivity through increased chemical inputs and mechanization

International Commission for the Protection of the Rhine against Pollution (IKSR)

International Joint Commission (IJC)

lagoon: a shallow, unlined pond where sunlight, bacterial action, algae and oxygen work to purify waste-water

leaching: the removal of soluble organic and inorganic substances from the topsoil downward by the action of percolating water

limiting nutrient: a chemical element necessary for growth, present in such small amounts that its availability determines the rate of growth

living machines: systems that use solar energy, aquaculture techniques and constructed wetlands to treat waste-water

mains: large sewers leading to a sewage treatment plant

multimedia pollution control: a holistic approach to pollution control that takes into account all environmental media (e.g. land, soil, air and water)

nitrate: the form of nitrogen taken up by plants; a common constituent of fertilizers nitrite: a form of nitrogen commonly created by bacterial action on nitrates

nitrogen: one of the primary nutrients responsible for eutrophication

non-point pollution: pollution of water bodies by diffuse sources over a widespread area such as agricultural or urban runoff, or atmospheric deposition

nutrients: as pollutants, any element or compound, such as phosphorus or nitrogen, that fuels eutrophication

organochlorines (chlorinated organic compounds, chlororganics): any organic compound that contains chlorine; includes many pesticides and industrial chemicals, such as DDT, PCBs, dioxins and furans

outfall: the mouth of a drain or sewer, where the contents discharge into a body of water

overland flow: a soil-based method of waste-water treatment in which waste-water flows over the surface of a relatively impermeable, vegetated slope

oxidation: a chemical reaction in which a compound loses an electron

ozonation: a method of disinfection that uses ozone, a powerful oxidant derived from oxygen

pathogens: organisms, such as certain bacteria and viruses, that cause disease

performance standards (or emission standards): standards that establish the amount of a particular pollutant that may be released to the environment

permeable: having pores or openings that allow water to pass through

persistent: refers to any toxic substance that remains in the environment for a significant period of time without breaking down

pesticides: substances used to prevent, destroy or repel a pest; includes herbicides, fungicides and insecticides phosphorus: one of the primary nutrients responsible for eutrophication

pit privy: a waterless toilet consisting essentially of a seat atop a hole in the ground

plume: the dispersion pattern made by the emissions from a pollution source as they spread out through the receiving medium

point source pollution: a source of pollutants that enter the environment at a single, distinct location, e.g. sewage outfall

polyaromatic hydrocarbons: aromatic hydrocarbons containing two or more benzene rings or other aromatic ring structures; environmentally persistent, often carcinogenic; emitted from a wide variety of sources

polychlorinated biphenols (PCBs): any of a class of organic compounds containing two or more chlorine atoms attached to an unbonded pair of benzene rings; mutagenic, carcinogenic, persistent and linked to delays in neurobehaviour development in infants; used in electrical and hydraulic equipment, lubricants and in many other fluids because they are chemically stable and heat resistant

precipitation: the process of solid particles settling out of a liquid

preliminary sewage treatment: the treatment of waste-water to remove materials that might create problems for the plant; includes bar screens to remove large floating debris, skimming tanks to remove floating oils and greases, and grit chambers to remove sand and other coarse settleable material

primary sewage treatment: an entirely physical process that settles out up to 40 per cent of organic wastes and 60 per cent of the solids from waste-water

pump and treat techniques: ground-water clean-up methods that involve removing contaminated ground-water from aquifers and treating it at the surface

rapid infiltration: a soil-based waste-water treatment system in which waste-water is applied intermittently to shallow basins or ponds, where it percolates into the surrounding soil receiving water: any watercourse or body of water into which waste-water or treated effluent is discharged

recharge: the process by which the water in an aquifer is replenished

restoration techniques: ground-water clean-up techniques that reduce pollution by removing the source of the pollution and/or decontaminating the polluted portion of the aquifer

retention time: a measure of the average time taken for waste-water to pass through a treatment unit

right-to-know legislation: legislation that forces companies to disclose any pollution or environmental risks they create

riparian: to do with the area immediately bordering a river or stream

runoff (also known as storm-water): overland flow of water caused by rainfall; often categorized as either urban or agricultural, depending where it occurs

sanitary sewer: an underground pipe that carries domestic sewage or industrial waste-water, but not storm-water

secondary sewage treatment: the biological treatment of waste-water to remove up to 85 per cent of BOD, most commonly by using either an activated sludge process or trickling filters

sediment: the fragmented organic or inorganic material derived from weathering of soil or rock

sedimentation: the process of sediment deposition

septic tank: a tank used to hold but not treat domestic wastes; common in rural areas

sewage farm: a farm that uses sewage for irrigation and fertilization, cleansing it in the process

slow-rate treatment: a soil-based waste-water treatment system in which waste-water is applied intermittently to vegetated land

sludge: in sanitary engineering, a semi-solid residue from sewage treatment processes solvent: a substance (usually liquid) capable of dissolving or dispersing other substances

specification standards (or design standards): standards that legislate the use of 'best available' technology for particular processes

storm sewer: a system of pipes that carry only water runoff from buildings and land surfaces

storm-water: see runoff

suspended solids (SS): any contaminant in water carried in suspension rather than being dissolved

tertiary sewage treatment: the advanced treatment of waste-water to levels beyond those reached by primary and secondary treatment; covers a wide variety of possible treatment processes including rapid sand filters, phosphorus removal, activated carbon and ion exchange; the particular process used will depend on the problem being addressed

Toxics Release Inventory (TRI)

tradable discharge permit (TDP): a government-issued permit, entitling the owner to discharge one unit of pollution during a specified time period, which can be traded between dischargers

trickling filter (also known as a clinker bed): a widely used method of secondary waste-water treatment in which waste-water is sprayed over a bed filled with rocks coated with algae, fungi and bacteria

turbidity: the cloudiness caused by the presence of suspended solids in water, limiting the depth to which light can penetrate

ultraviolet irradiation (UV irradiation): a method of waste-water disinfection that uses ultraviolet radiation to kill off pathogens

volatilization: the conversion of a chemical substance from a liquid form to a gas

water carriage: a water-based system of sewage disposal

watershed (also known as a drainage basin or catchment area): the geographic region drained by a river and its tributaries

watershed management: a pollution control policy encompassing a watershed water closet (WC)

wetlands: any area of land where the water table is at or near the surface of the land for a portion of the year long enough to support the growth of water-dependent vegetation such as reeds and cattails

Bibliography

Allen, Greg (1993) 'The Ways of Water: A Visit to the Boyne River School', in *Building With Water: New Approaches to Water Management* edited by Shigenori Suzuki; Furry Creek Alternative Centre, Vancouver

Brown, Lester et al (1996) *State of the World 1996* Earthscan Publications Ltd, London

Brix, H (1994) 'Functions of Macrophytes in Constructed Wetlands', *Water Science Technology* 29(4), pp76–78

Bulkley, Jonathan W (1995) 'Integrated Watershed Management: Past, Present and Future', *Water Resources Update* 100, pp7–18

Burke, Uwe and Peter C Lawrence (1990) 'A New Community Approach to Wastewater Treatment With Higher Water Plants', in P F Cooper and B C Findlater (eds) *Constructed Wetlands in Water Pollution Control* Pergamon Press, Oxford

Carson, Rachel (1962) *Silent Spring* Houghton Mifflin, Boston

The Conservation Foundation *Managing Agricultural Chemicals in the Environment*

Cooper, Kathy (1986) *The Great Lakes Primer* Pollution Probe, Toronto

Crombie, David (1992) *Regeneration: Toronto's Waterfront and the Sustainable City: Final Report* Royal Commission on the Future of the Toronto Waterfront, Toronto

ENDS Report 212 (1992) 'Water Companies See the UV Light on Sewage Disinfection' September

ENDS Report 243 (1995) 'Strategy Proposed for EC's Growing Sewage Sludge Mountain' April

EPA (US Environmental Protection Agency) (1989) *Managing Nonpoint Source Pollution: Final Report to Congress on Section 319 of the Clean Water Act (1989)* EPA/506/9-90 US EPA, Washington, DC

Feigin, A , I Rawina and J Shalhevet (1991) *Irrigation With Treated Sewage Effluent: Management for Environmental Protection* Springer-Verlag, Berlin

Finer, S E (1952) *The Life and Times of Sir Edwin Chadwick* Methuen and Co Ltd, London

GLUWQTF (Great Lakes United's Water Quality Task Force) (1987) *Unfulfilled Promises: A Citizen's Review of the International Great Lakes Water Quality Agreement* GLUWQTF, Buffalo

Government of Canada (1991) *The State of Canada's Environment* Government of Canada, Ottawa

Government of Canada (1993) *Canadian Environmental Protection Act: Priority Substances List Assessment Report* Government of Canada, Ottawa

Government of Canada (1995) *Pollution Prevention: A Federal Strategy for Action* Government of Canada, Ottawa

Hall, John and Clannat Howett (1994) 'Albemarle-Pamlico: Case Study in Pollutant Trading', *EPA Journal* Summer, pp27–29

Honachefsky, William B (1991) *Land Planner's Environmental Handbook* Noyes Publications, Pine Ridge, New Jersey

Huising, Donald, Larry Martin, Helene Hilger and Neil Seldman (1986) *Proven Profits from Pollution Prevention: Case Studies in Resource Conservation and Waste Reduction*, volume 1, Institute for Local Self-Reliance, Washington, DC

Hynes, H B N (1960) *The Biology of Polluted Waters* Liverpool University Press, Liverpool

Journal of the Institute of Water and Environmental Management (1992) October 6

Kadlec, Robert H and Robert L Knight (1996) *Treatment Wetlands* Lewis Publishers, Boca Raton, Florida

Kickuth, R (1970) 'Okochemische Leistungenttoherer Pflanzen', *Naturwiss* 57, pp55–61

Latham, Baldwin (1867) *A Lecture on the Sewage Difficulty* E & F N Spon, London

Loehr, Raymond C, William J Jewell, Joseph D Novak, William W Clarkson (1979) *Land Application of Wastes*, 1, Van Nostrand Rheinhold, New York

Mollison, Bill (1988) *Permaculture: A Designer's Manual* Tagari Publications, Tyalgum, Australia

NRC (National Research Council) (1992) *Alternatives for Groundwater Cleanup* Rheinhold, Washington, DC

NRC (1996) *Use of Reclaimed Water and Sludge in Food Crop Production* National Academy Press, Washington, DC

OECD (1994) *OECD Environmental Indicators* OECD, Paris

Olson, Richard K (1993) *Created and Natural Wetlands for Controlling Nonpoint Source Pollution* C K Smoley, Boca Raton, Florida

Organic Gardening (1997) 'Rodale Proves Organic Works', 44(4), pp20–21

Post, James E (1994) 'Environmental Approaches and Strategies: Regulation, Markets, and Management Education', in Rao V Kolluru (ed) *Environmental Strategies Handbook: A Guide to Effective Policies and Practices* McGraw Hill, New York

Pries, John H (1994) *Wastewater and Stormwater Applications of Wetlands in Canada* North American Wetlands Conservation Council, Ottawa

Reed, Sherwood C and Donald S Brown (1992) 'Constructed Wetland Design – The First Generation' *Water Environment Research* 64 (6) pp776–781

Reed, Sherwood C, Ronald W Crites and E Joe Middlebrooks (1995) *Natural Systems for Waste Management and Treatment* second edition, McGraw Hill, New York

Riggle, David (1996) 'Technology Improves for Composting Toilets' *Bicycle* April 1996 pp39–43

Riggs, David W (1993) *Market Incentive for Water Quality: A Case Study of the Tar–Pamlico River Basin, North Carolina* Center for Policy Studies, Clemson, South Carolina

Roechling, Herman Alfred (1892) 'The Sewage Farms of Berlin', *Minutes of the Proceedings of the Institution of Civil Engineering 109*

Sedgwick, William T (1918) *Principles of Sanitary Science and the Public Health* New York

Seidel, K, Happel H and G Graue (1978) *Contributions to Revitalisation of Waters* second edition, Siftung Limnologische Arbeitsgruppe Dr Siedel eV, Krefeld, Germany

Shaeffer, John R and Leonard A Stevens (1983) *Future Water* William Morrow & Co, New York

Sincero, Arcadio P, Sr and Gregoria A Sincero (1996) *Environmental Engineering: A Design Approach* Prentice Hall, Upper Saddle River, New Jersey

Singh, Bijay and G S Sekhon (1978–9) 'Nitrate Pollution of Groundwater from Farm Use of Nitrogen Fertilizers – A Review', *Agriculture and Environment* 4, pp207–25

Southe, Judith D and Jon K Piper (1992) *Farming in Nature's Image: An Ecological Approach to Agriculture* Island Press, Washington, DC

Spencer, Robert (1990) 'Solar Aquatic Treatment of Septage', *BioCycle* May, pp66–70

Stanners, David and Philippe Bordeau (1995) *Europe's Environment: The Döbris Assessment* Earthscan/European Environment Agency, London/Copenhagen

Symposium on the Inter-Parliamentary Union (1979) *Environment in Europe: Air and Water Pollution, Including Transboundary Flows* Union Interparlementaire, Geneva

Waddell, Thomas E and Blair T Bower (1988) *Managing Agricultural Chemicals in the Environment: The Case for a Multimedia Approach* The Conservation Foundation, Washington, DC

WWF (1995) 'Toxics That Tamper With Hormones', *Eagle's Eye*, Summer

Index

also published by

ECOLOGY OF EVERYDAY LIFE
Rethinking the Desire for Nature
Chaia Heller

Ecology of Everyday Life examines the ecological impulse as a 'desire for nature,' a desire that emerges as people within industrial capitalist contexts respond to the personal and aesthetic, rather than the physical and political implications of ecological breakdown.

While exploring the historical causes of this romantic 'desire for nature,' Heller also offers a way to reconstruct ideas of both 'nature' and 'desire,' drawing from feminist, anarchist, and social ecological theory. She provides an activist response to ecological questions, linking the desire for a more meaningful and integral quality of life to the activist impulse itself.

> *In a lively style, and from a social-ecological perspective that is free of the mysticism so much in vogue today, Heller provides an incisive discussion on the ideas of desire and everyday life. This is an exciting, provocative, and truly insightful work.*
> **Murray Bookchin**

> *Heller brings back the joy and spontaneity to activism, reminding us that the struggle for freedom and justice is not a duty or a chore: rather, this struggle articulates our deepest desires as social creatures.*
> **Greta Gaard, *Ecological Politics: Ecofeminists and the Greens***

> *For ways to rethink and remake the world, read this book.*
> **Carolyn Merchant, *Death of Nature* and *Earthcare: Women and the Environment***

Chaia Heller holds a MA in psychology and has worked for many years as a clinical social worker counselling and advocating for women struggling with issues of domestic abuse and poverty. In addition, she has had a long career as a teacher and international lecturer in the fields of social ecology and ecofeminism and is currently on the faculty at the Institute for Social Ecology.

204 pages, bibliography, index
Paperback ISBN: 1-55164-132-1 $19.99
Hardcover ISBN: 1-55164-133-X $48.99

MURRAY BOOKCHIN READER

Janet Biehl, editor

This collection provides an overview of the thought of the foremost social theorist and political philosopher of the libertarian left today. His writings span five decades, and subject matter of remarkable breadth. Bookchin's writings on revolutionary philosophy, politics, and history are far less known than the specific controversies that have surrounded him, but they are deserving of far greater attention.

Despite his critical engagement with both Marxism and anarchism, his political philosophy, known as 'libertarian municipalism', draws on the best of both for the emancipatory tools to build a democratic libertarian alternative. His nature philosophy is an organic outlook of generation, development, and evolution, that grounds human beings in natural evolution, yet, contrary to today's fashionable antihuman-ism, places them firmly at its summit. Bookchin's anthropological writings trace the rise of hierarchy and domination out of egalitarian societies, while his historical writings cover important chapters in the European revolutionary tradition.

The selections in this reader constitute a sampling from the writings of one of the pivotal thinkers of our era.

Janet Biehl is also the author of *Finding Our Way: Rethinking Ecofeminist Politics*, and, with Murray Bookchin, *Politics of Social Ecology*, both published by Black Rose Books. She lectures at the Insti-tute of Social Ecology in Plainfield, Vermont.

Murray Bookchin, Professor Emeritus at the School of Environ-mental Studies, Ramapo College and Director Emeritus of the Insti-tute of Social Ecology, has authored more than a dozen books on urbanism, ecology, technology and philosophy. For those interested in exploring more deeply his ideas, Black Rose Books has published nine of these titles.

> 288 pages, bibliography, index
> Paperback ISBN: 1-55164-118-6 $24.99
> Hardcover ISBN: 1-55164-119-4 $53.99

Titles by this Murray Bookchin include:

Defending the Earth   *Post-Scarcity Anarchism*
Ecology of Freedom   *Remaking Society*
Limits of the City   *Toward an Ecological Society*
Modern Crisis   *Urbanization Without Cities*
Philosophy of Social Ecology

BLACK ROSE BOOKS

has also published the following books of related interest

Anarchism and Ecology, *by Graham Purchase*
Beyond Boundaries, *by Barbara Noske*
Ecology of The Automobile, *by Peter Freund, George Martin*
Finding Our Way: Rethinking Eco-Feminist Politics, *by Janet Biehl*
Green Guerrillas, *by Helen Collinson, editor*
Intertwining, *by John Grande*
Murray Bookchin Reader, *by Janet Biehl and Murray Bookchin*
Nature and the Crisis of Modernity, *by Raymond Rogers*
Oceans Are Emptying, *by Raymond Rogers*
Political Ecology, *by Dimitrios Roussopoulos*
Politics of Social Ecology, *by Janet Biehl and Murray Bookchin*
Politics of Sustainable Development, *by Laurie E. Adkin*
Philosophy of Social Ecology, *by Murray Bookchin*
Race, Class, Women and the State, *by Tanya Schecter*
Rethinking Camelot, *by Noam Chomsky*
Solving History, *by Raymond Rogers*
Sustainability—The Challenge, *by L. Anders Sandberg, Sverker Sörlin, editors*
Triumph of the Market, *by Edward S. Herman*
Women Pirates, *by Ulrike Klausmann, Marion Meinzerin, Gabriel Kuhn*
Women and Religion, *by Fatmagül Berktay*

send for a free catalogue of all our titles
BLACK ROSE BOOKS
C.P. 1258, Succ. Place du Parc
Montréal, Québec
H3W 2R3 Canada

or visit our web site at: http://www.web.net/blackrosebooks
To order books in North America:
(phone) 1-800-565-9523   (fax) 1-800-221-9985
In Europe: (phone) 44-0181-986-4854 (fax) 44-0181-533-5821

Printed by the workers of
MARC VEILLEUX IMPRIMEUR INC.
Boucherville, Quebec
for Black Rose Books Ltd.

The Water Crisis